LONGMAN CRITICAL ESSAYS

ROMEO AND JULIET

William Shakespeare

Editors:
Linda Cookson
Bryan Loughrey

Longman Critical Essays

Editors: Linda Cookson and Bryan Loughrey

Titles in the series:

Antony and Cleopatra   0 582 06051 6
Emma   0 582 00653 8
The General Prologue to the Canterbury Tales   0 582 03790 5
Hamlet   0 582 00648 1
Julius Caesar   0 582 07579 3
Keats   0 582 00652 X
Philip Larkin   0 582 03810 3
King Lear   0 582 00649 X
Macbeth   0 582 00650 3
Measure for Measure   0 582 07576 9
The Merchant of Venice   0 582 07575 0
The Metaphysical Poets   0 582 06048 6
A Midsummer Night's Dream   0 582 07580 7
Much Ado About Nothing   0 582 03791 3
Othello   0 582 07578 5
The Pardoner's Prologue and Tale   0 582 06049 4
Richard II   0 582 03792 1
Romeo and Juliet   0 582 07577 7
The Tempest   0 582 00651 1
Twelfth Night   0 582 06050 8
The Waste Land   0 582 00655 4
Wuthering Heights   0 582 00654 6

CONTENTS

Preface   5

Introduction: How to use this volume   7

Essays   9

Sexual politics
Cedric Watts   9

'My grave is like to be my wedding bed':
stage, text and performance
Graham Holderness   19

The tragic potential of comedy
Peter Hollindale   30

The Fourth Man
John E Cunningham   42

The 'yoke of stars': power and compulsion
Michael Spiller   52

'Whining poetry':
Romeo and Juliet and love poetry
Michael Mangan   63

Time and art
John Saunders   75

Blind Cupid and death
Susie Campbell   85

Fate, responsibility and blame
Angus Alton 94

The language of love
Marilyn Powrie 105

A practical guide to essay writing 113

Introduction 113

How to plan an essay 114

Style sheet 125

Suggestions for further reading 131

Like all professional groups, literary critics have developed their own specialised language. This is not necessarily a bad thing. Sometimes complex concepts can only be described in a terminology far removed from everyday speech. Academic jargon, however, creates an unnecessary barrier between the critic and the intelligent but less practised reader.

This danger is particularly acute where scholarly books and articles are re-packaged for a student audience. Critical anthologies, for example, often contain extracts from longer studies originally written for specialists. Deprived of their original context, these passages can puzzle and at times mislead. The essays in this volume, however, are all specially commissioned, self-contained works, written with the needs of students firmly in mind.

This is not to say that the contributors — all experienced critics and teachers — have in any way attempted to simplify the complexity of the issues with which they deal. On the contrary, they explore the central problems of the text from a variety of critical perspectives, reaching conclusions which are challenging and at times mutually contradictory.

They try, however, to present their arguments in a direct, accessible language and to work within the limitations of scope and length which students inevitably face. For this reason, essays are generally rather briefer than is the practice; they address quite specific topics; and, in line with examination requirements, they incorporate precise textual detail into the body of the discussion.

They offer, therefore, working examples of the kind of essay-writing skills which students themselves are expected to develop. Their diversity, however, should act as a reminder that in the field of literary studies there is no such thing as a 'model' answer. Good essays are the outcome of a creative engagement with literature, of sensitive, attentive reading and careful thought. We hope that those contained in this volume will encourage students to return to the most important starting point of all, the text itself, with renewed excitement and the determination to explore more fully their own critical responses.

How to use this volume

Obviously enough, you should start by reading the text in question. The one assumption that all the contributors make is that you are already familiar with this. It would be helpful, of course, to have read further — perhaps other works by the same author or by influential contemporaries. But we don't assume that you have yet had the opportunity to do this and any references to historical background or to other works of literature are explained.

You should, perhaps, have a few things to hand. It is always a good idea to keep a copy of the text nearby when reading critical studies. You will almost certainly want to consult it when checking the context of quotations or pausing to consider the validity of the critic's interpretation. You should also try to have access to a good dictionary, and ideally a copy of a dictionary of literary terms as well. The contributors have tried to avoid jargon and to express themselves clearly and directly. But inevitably there will be occasional words or phrases with which you are unfamiliar. Finally, we would encourage you to make notes, summarising not just the argument of each essay but also your own responses to what you have read. So keep a pencil and notebook at the ready.

Suitably equipped, the best thing to do is simply begin with whichever topic most interests you. We have deliberately organised each volume so that the essays may be read in any order. One consequence of this is that, for the sake of clarity and self-containment, there is occasionally a degree of overlap between essays. But at least you are not forced to follow one — fairly arbitrary — reading sequence.

Each essay is followed by brief 'Afterthoughts', designed to highlight points of critical interest. But remember, these are only there to remind you that it is *your* responsibility to question what you read. The essays printed here are not a series of 'model' answers to be slavishly imitated and in no way should they be regarded as anything other than a guide or stimulus for your own thinking. We hope for a critically involved response: 'That was interesting. But if *I* were tackling the topic . . . !'

Read the essays in this spirit and you'll pick up many of the skills of critical composition in the process. We have, however, tried to provide more explicit advice in 'A practical guide to essay writing'. You may find this helpful, but do not imagine it offers any magic formulas. The quality of your essays ultimately depends on the quality of your engagement with literary texts. We hope this volume spurs you on to read these with greater understanding and to explore your responses in greater depth.

A note on the text

All references are to the New Penguin Shakespeare edition of *Romeo and Juliet*, ed. T J B Spencer

Cedric Watts

Cedric Watts is Professor of English at
Sussex University, and the author of
many scholarly publications.

ESSAY

Sexual politics

Romeo and Juliet has, historically, proved to be an immensely successful and influential play. In the twentieth century, for example, its influence has been exerted through stage productions, films for cinema and television, videos, radio, records, tapes, cassettes, adaptations and modernisations (including ballets, operas and musicals), parodies, burlesques, cartoons, and even bank-notes — as, for a while, the lovers lent incongruous grace to the British twenty-pound note. Even people who have never read the play are likely to know of Romeo and Juliet as famed exemplars of tragic romantic love. Familiarity may breed not contempt but blinkered appreciation. The play is so well known that we may take its sexual politics for granted; and we may therefore overlook the extent to which its political influence, over the centuries, has been predominantly progressive. By 'progressive' I mean 'congenial to liberal rather than illiberal outlooks'. In this essay, I discuss three aspects of its sexual politics. First, the feministic features. Second, the advocacy of marriage based on the free choice of loving partners. Third, the capture of religious rhetoric by secular individualism.

1

Although Juliet is only thirteen years old, she displays a precociously independent intelligence. Consider the famous 'orchard' scene, in which Romeo, standing in the garden, addresses Juliet on her balcony. Romeo attempts to offer the conventional rhetoric of the ardent lover:

> Lady, by yonder blessèd moon I vow,
> That tips with silver all these fruit-tree tops
>
> (II.2.107–108)

— but is at once checked by Juliet:

> O swear not by the moon, th'inconstant moon,
> That monthly changes in her circled orb,
> Lest that thy love prove likewise variable.
>
> (II.2.109–111)

Romeo, temporarily baffled by this shrewd rebuke, asks 'What shall I swear by?'; and she replies:

> Do not swear at all.
> Or if thou wilt, swear by thy gracious self,
> Which is the god of my idolatry,
> And I'll believe thee.
>
> (II.2.112–115)

Romeo starts again with 'If my heart's dear love' — and is again checked when she says:

> Well, do not swear. Although I joy in thee,
> I have no joy of this contract tonight.
> It is too rash, too unadvised, too sudden;
> Too like the lightning, which doth cease to be
> Ere one can say 'It lightens'.
>
> (II.2.116–120)

Her forebodings prove accurate, since their love will indeed be short-lived: the duration of the play's action is just under four days, from Sunday morning to dawn on Thursday. What is notable in the quoted exchange is that Juliet is shrewdly critical of conventional amatory rhetoric; and it is criticism that Romeo needs. Although Romeo is probably several years older than Juliet, it is he who seems relatively immature and callow. His protestations of undying love for Rosaline abruptly give place to his fuller love for Juliet; and it is Juliet, not Romeo, who decisively presses the courtship towards marriage:

> If that thy bent of love be honourable,
> Thy purpose marriage, send me word tomorrow,
> By one that I'll procure to come to thee,
> Where and what time thou wilt perform the rite
>
> (II.2.143–146)

So, although she says that she will regard him as her 'lord', the play gives the impression that Juliet is actually shrewder and more decisive than is Romeo. Dramatically, greater emphasis falls finally on her than on him, for she is given the theatrical accolade of the later death.

The lovers' deaths have many causes; and a prominent cause is, of course, the feud. That feud seems to have no substantial origin (the Prince says that its 'Three civil brawls' were 'bred of an airy word', I.1.89) and is sustained by the menfolk: it is they, not the women, who seek a pretext for fighting. This point is established in the play's first scene, when both Capulet and Montague, though old, are foolishly eager to join the fray, and are symmetrically rebuked by their wives. Lady Capulet cries mockingly: 'A crutch, a crutch! Why call you for a sword?' (line 76); Lady Montague tells her husband: 'Thou shalt not stir one foot to seek a foe' (line 80). The opening sequence, in which Sampson and Gregory provoke the public brawl, clearly establishes that men who maintain the feud have a naïve and immature conception of masculinity; in relationships with other men and with women, aggressiveness is thought to be meritorious. Sampson's jocular boasting is symptomatic:

> ... women, being the weaker vessels, are ever thrust to the wall. Therefore I will push Montague's men from the wall, and thrust his maids to the wall.
>
> (I.1.14–17)

In contrast, the play offers a different conception of masculinity: one in which the relationship with a woman is characterised by loving mutuality, not lustful force, and the relationship with other men is constructive and pacific, rather than violent. Romeo, newly married to Juliet, seeks to be a peace-maker; but then, at a crucial moment, he foolishly (if understandably) opts for the aggressive rather than the pacific conception of masculinity. When Mercutio has been killed by Tybalt, Romeo says:

> O sweet Juliet,
> Thy beauty hath made me effeminate
> And in my temper softened valour's steel!

(III.1.113–115)

Here he wrongly (and, in the event, tragically) deems the pacific sense of masculinity an 'effeminate' enfeeblement. He therefore opts for the aggressive sense of masculinity, challenges and slays Tybalt, and is consequently exiled; the further confusions and the deaths of the lovers ensue. We could say, then, that the tragedies of Romeo and Juliet are a consequence of the choice of a primitive definition of the masculine instead of a more civilised definition.

In their love, Romeo and Juliet had disregarded the claims of clan and family. By their deaths, they end the feud. The older generation (including even the Prince)[1] stands rebuked by the example of the lovers who prefer union in death to the division which was enforced by the patriarchal clan-system.

2

These days, most young people in the western world take it for granted that marriage should be based on the free choice of loving partners. This orthodoxy was once a heterodoxy. *Romeo and Juliet* helped the modern view to triumph over the older view, which was that the choice of partners should (at least among the well-to-do) be made by the older members of the families concerned. In his historical study, *The Family, Sex and*

---

[1] The Prince says: 'I, for winking at your discords too, / Have lost a brace of kinsmen. All are punished.' (V.3.294–295).

Marriage in England 1500–1800 (London, 1977), Lawrence Stone declares:

> Until romanticism triumphed in the late eighteenth century, there was . . . a clear conflict of values between the idealization of love by some poets, playwrights and the authors of romances on the one hand, and its rejection as a form of imprudent folly and even madness by all theologians, moralists, authors of manuals of conduct, and parents and adults in general. Everyone knew about it, some experienced it, but only a minority of young courtiers made it a way of life, and even they did not necessarily regard it as a suitable basis for a life-long marriage . . . To an Elizabethan audience the tragedy of Romeo and Juliet, like that of Othello, lay not so much in their ill-starred romance as in the way they brought destruction upon themselves by violating the norms of the society in which they lived, which in the former case meant strict filial obedience and loyalty to the traditional friendships and enmities of the lineage. An Elizabethan courtier would be familiar enough with the bewitching passion of love to feel some sympathy with the young couple, but he would see clearly enough where duty lay.
>
> (pp. 181, 187)

These comments seem to imply that the bitter and racially prejudiced Brabantio, whose daughter leaves him to marry a Moor, represents the moral centre of the tragedy *Othello*, and that the domineering Capulet of Act III scene 5 of *Romeo and Juliet* is wiser than the chastened, forgiving Capulet of the play's close. Lawrence Stone himself notes that various young Elizabethan noblemen married in defiance of their relatives' plans, and sometimes were jailed or disinherited as a result; while Ralph Houlbrooke's study, *The English Family* (London and New York, 1984), observes that such marriages for love were more frequent than Stone concedes. Certainly, the pressures of family and clan, of business and trade, of convenience in work, must often have prevailed against romantic desires when partners in marriage were being chosen; but the very popularity, at all levels of society, of the literature of romance strongly suggests that the claims of personal ardour were increasingly being weighed against the claims of prudence and economic practicality. In the long battle between the rival ideas of a sound basis for marriage, Shakespeare's plays – and *Romeo and Juliet* in particular — have resonantly voiced the idea which eventually prevailed. Furthermore, Germaine Greer has argued that in exalting the principle of wedlock based on love, in opposition to the Catholic view that celibacy was a more honourable state than marriage, Shakespeare's originality may be overlooked:

> ... it is not easy for us to estimate Shakespeare's originality in developing the idea of the complementary couple as the linchpin of the social structure. The medieval Church regarded marriage as a second-rate condition ... Shakespeare took up the cudgels on the side of the reformers ... He projected the ideal of the monogamous heterosexual couple so luminously [in his writings] that they irradiate our notions of compatibility and co-operation between spouses to this day.[2]

3

The ideal of marriage based on the free choice of loving partners is, historically, a relatively recent phenomenon, and more local-ised geographically than we may at first think. Margaret Mead, the anthropologist, remarked in her famous study, *Coming of Age in Samoa* (Harmondsworth, 1943):

> Samoans rate romantic fidelity in terms of days or weeks at most and are inclined to scoff at tales of lifelong devotion. (They greeted the story of Romeo and Juliet with incredulous contempt.)
>
> (p. 11)

CS Lewis's influential work, *The Allegory of Love* (New York, 1958), argued that the ideal of romantic love emerged in medieval Europe, burgeoned between the Elizabethan and the Victorian age, and came under attack (potentially fatal attack) from Freudians, feminists and others in the twentieth century. Freudianism suggested that this ideal is merely a sublimation of

---

[2] Germaine Greer, *Shakespeare* (Oxford, 1986), pp. 121, 124.

an impeded libidinal desire: a cultural sophistication of sexual lust. Marxists claimed that the ideal emerged as a consequence of the bourgeois economic system:

> ... for inherited customs and historical rights it substituted purchase and sale, 'free' contract ...
>
> But the closing of contracts presupposes people who can freely dispose of their persons, actions and possessions, and who meet each other on equal terms.
>
> ... In short, love marriage was proclaimed a human right[3]

Accordingly, in David Lodge's recent novel, *Nice Work* (London, 1989), the heroine, who is a Marxist-feminist lecturer, reproaches the man who declares love for her:

> 'There's no such thing ... It's a rhetorical device. It's a bourgeois fallacy.'
>
> (p. 293)

The play itself anticipates those later sceptical appraisals of romantic love. The Freudian emphasis on romantic love as a sublimation of impeded desire could be related to the barriers which impede the union of Romeo and Juliet: the orchard wall which is 'hard to climb', the high balcony, the feud dividing their families, the sentence of exile, the tomb's iron gates, and the ultimate barrier of death. Mercutio is a Freudian when he says: 'Prick love for pricking and you beat love down' (I.4.28). (In other words, 'Gratify lust and you overcome love.') The Marxist association of the '"free" contract' of marriage with the bourgeois economy could be illustrated by Romeo and Juliet, since both belong to the prosperous burgher class, and, in addition, the language of 'purchase and sale' is evident in Juliet's desire at its most ardent:

> O I have bought the mansion of a love,
> But not possessed it; and though I am sold,
> Not yet enjoyed.
>
> (III.2.26–28)

---

[3] Karl Marx and Friedrich Engels, *Selected Works*, vol. II (Moscow, 1958), pp. 238, 239.

The notion that love is merely 'a rhetorical device', a construct of language, lacking solid substance, is suggested by the rhetoric of Romeo's protestations of love for Rosaline and particularly by Mercutio's mockery:

> Now is he for the numbers that Petrarch flowed in. Laura, to his lady, was a kitchen wench . . . this drivelling love is . . . like a great natural that runs lolling up and down to hide his bauble in a hole.
>
> (II.4.38–40, 89–90)

Clearly, one reason for the resilience, the liveliness and the cultural durability of *Romeo and Juliet* is that alongside the famed sweetness of its lyrical affirmations flows the salt and vinegar of its cynical bawdry. Repeatedly the play asks: Which is truer, the enhancive definition of love which is implicit in the relationship of Romeo and Juliet themselves, or the reductive definition of love which is implicit in the bawdry of Mercutio, the Nurse, Sampson, Gregory and Peter? The play voices scepticism but is intelligent enough to be sceptical about that scepticism. The uncompromising amatory idealism of Romeo and Juliet leads to their deaths; but the most intelligent representative of the reductive view of love is Mercutio, and his spirit of sceptical mockery brings him, also, to an early grave. The ideal of romantic love propagated by the play's hero and heroine may, in reality, have brought as much misery as happiness, because it sets standards of emotional intensity which, in life, may seldom be durably attained. The sceptical notion that heterosexual love is basically a matter of hedonistic carnality is vigorously voiced by the play's comic figures; and, in reality, such a notion may have brought as much misery as pleasure, because it tends to degrade human individuality. The strength of *Romeo and Juliet* lies in that mutually critical interplay of the enhancive and reductive conceptions of love. That is why the play, though so richly lyrical, remains predominantly unsentimental; and that is why, if cultural scepticism prevails, *Romeo and Juliet* will remain cogently and challengingly relevant.

As we have noted, Juliet says to Romeo, '. . . swear by thy gracious self,/ Which is the god of my idolatry'; and, later, she poignantly declares:

My bounty is as boundless as the sea,
My love as deep. The more I give to thee,
The more I have, for both are infinite.

(II.2.133–135)

When courtly lovers like Romeo addressed their ladies as goddesses or saints, and when heroines like Juliet addressed their wooers as gods or pilgrims; when the goal of aspiration became not an infinity of otherworldly bliss in the heaven promised by Christianity to the virtuous worshipper of God, but the infinity of love which mortal lovers promised each other here on earth; then a revolution was taking place. The language of religion was being captured and redirected to express a newly exalted conception of human individuality and of sexual mutuality. For better and sometimes for worse, the consequences of that revolution remain with us today. If, like David Lodge's heroine, we feel sceptical about 'the discourse of romantic love', we should perhaps note that in *Romeo and Juliet* such scepticism is associated with a hedonism which is often entertaining but is sometimes aggressive, male-chauvinistic and destructive.

AFTERTHOUGHTS

1

What do you understand by 'feministic' (page 9)?

2

Would the Montagues and the Capulets have been wise, in your view, to allow their son and daughter to marry?

3

How relevant do you find a consideration of Freudian or Marxist theory to a study of *Romeo and Juliet*?

4

What distinction does Watts draw between an 'enhancive' and a 'reductive' definition of love (page 16)?

Graham Holderness

Graham Holderness is Head of the Drama Department at Roehampton Institute, and has published numerous works of criticism.

ESSAY

'My grave is like to be my wedding bed': stage, text and performance

The purpose of this essay is to imagine, through a combination of historical reconstruction and textual analysis, some aspects of an Elizabethan performance of *Romeo and Juliet*. In what kind of theatre was it first produced? The typical Elizabethan public playhouse of the period was a circular, open-air building, containing a big platform stage partially covered by a tiled roof. Within a round or polygonal structure the stage occupied a central position. At the rear of the stage stood a flat wall, behind which was the 'tiring-house' (where the actors 'attired') surmounted by a gallery. Exits and entrances were made through two doors in the tiring-house façade; above the doors there was the gallery, in which actors could appear 'aloft'. The physical resources available to the players were thus basically very simple: a bare, flat stage; two doors for entrances and exits, and a playing area 'aloft'. The stage had no movable scenery, and no artificial lighting: the visual setting therefore remained virtually the same, except for the use of props, for every production; and the performances were lit by ordinary daylight.

Let us then attempt to locate the play-text we have before us into the physical space of this type of theatre. Consider first the question of *location*. Where do events actually happen in this play? The Elizabethan theatres used a bare stage without scenery: so there was no representation of *place* as there often is in modern theatres, or in film or television adaptations. At the beginning of Act I scene 2, we would naturally assume that Capulet and Paris are conversing in the former's house. The servant doesn't actually go anywhere: Capulet and Paris go out leaving him alone on stage. When Benvolio and Romeo appear and meet him, it becomes obvious that this certainly can't be Capulet's house. When in the eighteenth century scholars began to edit Elizabethan play-texts, editors would often supply a location: Edward Capell for example, publishing an edition of the plays in 1768, got around this difficulty by prescribing *'Verona, a street'* as the location of the whole scene, and many subsequent editions followed suit. This provides a natural enough place in which Romeo and Benvolio can meet the Clown: but it seems correspondingly awkward to assume that Capulet should discuss his daughter's marriage with a distinguished suitor in the street too!

In the Elizabethan theatres, this didn't really present a problem at all. Since the stage didn't represent any particular place, it could be imagined as representing any place necessary or convenient for the scene. An Elizabethan audience would have been quite happy to think of the earlier part of the scene taking place in Capulet's house, and then to assume that the location had changed to a street before the Clown meets Romeo and Benvolio. Simply by walking across the stage, the Clown could suggest a change of location, without the visible appearance of the stage changing at all.

Later in Act I, scene 4, Romeo, Mercutio and their companions talk about gate-crashing Capulet's feast. They are carrying torches, partly to indicate that the scene is set at night. At the end of their conversation, they don't however leave the stage to undertake that journey; they perform instead a pantomimic trip around the stage to the Capulet house. The

Elizabethan texts show that the Montagues didn't actually go off, but remained on stage: *'They march about the stage'*. The Capulet servants simultaneously bring on the properties of the feast: *'They march about the stage; and Servingmen come forth with napkins'*. When the Capulets enter, the stage direction makes it clear that the disguised Montagues stay where they are, and the Capulets come forward to greet them: *'Enter Capulet, his wife, Juliet, Tybalt, Nurse, and all the guests and gentlewomen to the maskers'*. The Montagues stay where they are, the Capulet servants bring in the feast, the family and other guests arrive by entering the stage area — the Montagues don't go to the feast, the feast comes to them. In an Elizabethan performance, in other words, the revellers would simply walk around the stage to indicate that they were 'going somewhere' — i.e. walking to, and entering, Capulet's house. Again, eighteenth-century editors would substitute for the original stage directions an *'Exeunt'*, clearing the stage so that the Capulet feast could be staged by a re-setting of the scene, moving the location into Capulet's house. More modern editions, like the Penguin Shakespeare text, go back to the original texts, use their stage directions, and prescribe no fixed locations for individual scenes.

We are today accustomed to dramatic media such as television and film, which represent locations directly and unmistakably, by filming their physical equivalents — a city, a domestic interior, a forest, a sea-shore. The editors of the eighteenth and nineteenth centuries, who laid the basis for our modern Shakespeare texts, were accustomed to a theatre in which location was established by the use of pictorial scenery, and maintained by frequent and elaborate scene-changes. Hence eighteenth- and nineteenth-century texts prescribe different locations, and imply theatrical scene-changes, within their construction of the dramatic narrative.

Let us look for example at the last 'movement' of the play, which begins with Juliet taking the poison (in IV.3). In an Elizabethan theatre in or around the 1590s, the stage would not have changed its appearance at all throughout this sequence of events. That of course is standard practice and nothing unusual. What makes this sequence particularly remarkable is the fact that Juliet's drugged and unconscious body was obviously intended to *remain on stage* throughout the rest of the play. The location of the performance alters to somewhere else in the Capulet house (IV.4), back to Juliet's bedroom (IV.5), to Romeo in Mantua (V.1), to Friar Laurence's cell (V.2), to the Capulet monument (V.3). But in Elizabethan stagings, Juliet clearly remained on stage: at the end of IV.3, where the second Quarto text gives no stage direction, and the Folio gives *'Exit'* (a direction which would, if followed, commit the actress to a clumsy stagger off stage), the first Quarto states precisely: *'She falls upon her bed, within the curtains'*.

Precisely *where* on the stage she would have rested, requires further discussion and comment. Much scholarly discussion of the staging of Elizabethan plays has worked on the assumption that the theatres had, in addition to the resources detailed above, an inner stage or 'discovery space' at the back of the platform stage, recessed into the 'tiring-house', which could have been closed off from the main stage by curtains. Such an additional space would make the above sequence of scenes relatively easy to organise: Juliet would actually disappear from view of the audience by falling through the curtains onto a 'bed' inside the recessed inner stage. Subsequent scenes like IV.4 could then have been played with those curtains closed, and Juliet completely hidden. The Nurse would have 'discovered' her sleeping (apparently dead) form by drawing back the curtains. Closing them again would leave the stage clear for V.1 and V.2, and in V.3 they could be drawn again to symbolise the opening of the Capulet tomb.

My view is that there was no such 'inner stage', at least in the theatre where and when *Romeo and Juliet* was originally performed. Without an inner stage, Juliet's bed would have had to be, and to remain, on the main stage, and scenes like IV.4, V.1 and V.2 played under the conventional pretence that the characters on stage would be unaware of the heroine lying there, unconscious and partly concealed. The 'curtains' would be curtains around the bed, not stage-curtains fencing off a separate acting area. That pattern of staging would require a non-naturalistic method of performance, in which the bed and its occupant could be excluded from, or brought into view, according to the requirements of the dramatic narrative. Even if there was an inner stage, this scene could still not have worked naturalistically, since the same physical object would have had to change its significance from one scene to another, beginning as a piece of furniture in a girl's bedroom, and ending as a bier in her family vault. So the physical resources of the stage clearly worked in a symbolic, emblematic way rather than, like the stage technology of later theatres, aiming at a convincing 'realism' of dramatic presentation.

In the Penguin Shakespeare text of *Romeo and Juliet*, the action is divided into scenes as follows:

IV.3   Juliet drinks the potion.

IV.4   Capulets prepare for the wedding.

IV.5   Nurse discovers Juliet 'dead'.

V.1   Balthasar tells Romeo of Juliet's 'death'. Romeo buys poison from the Apothecary.

V.2   Friar Laurence meets Friar John, and learns of the disastrous miscarriage of the message.

V.3   Paris enters the churchyard; Romeo appears and breaks open the tomb, kills Paris, commits suicide. Juliet wakes, finds Romeo dead, kills herself. The Prince and the two families arrive to find them dead.

Although this text does not fix the scenes in particular locations, it still divides some sequences into separate scenes, even though in fact the normal principle of scene-division — that the stage is cleared and other characters enter — does not apply. Most of the original texts — including the second Quarto and the Folio — have no scene divisions at all. The first Quarto indicates a break between sections of narrative, at the points where later editors made scene-divisions, by inserting a row of printer's ornaments between the passages of text. This device would have told the actors where a change of stage personnel occurred: but it did not of course carry the same implications as a modern 'change of scene'. Eighteenth-century editors formalised those breaks into scene-divisions to accommodate the play to their own type of theatre, where scene-shifts would actually be made by the changing of pictorial scenery. Thus in eighteenth-century editions of the play, and in later editions which followed them, you would find these now separate scenes set in different locations.

IV.3   *Juliet's Chamber*
IV.4   *A Hall*
IV.4   SCENE *changes to Juliet's chamber,* Juliet *on a bed.*
V.1   *Mantua. A street.*
V.2   *Verona. Friar Laurence's cell.*
V.3   *Verona; a churchyard; in it a tomb belonging to the*
        Capulets

None of this could have applied to the Elizabethan stage, where locations could not have been fixed in this way. They only make sense for a theatre where movable scenery supplies location by the visual representation of a particular place. The introductory stage direction of the eighteenth-century text for IV.4 actually states that the *'SCENE changes':* in an eighteenth-century theatre this would have involved a painted backcloth being drawn aside to reveal another one. Another eighteenth-century edition has a different direction for this passage: *Ante-room of Juliet's chamber. Door of the Chamber open, and* Juliet *upon her bed.* To stage this conception a theatre would have to be able to construct the appearance of two separate rooms on the stage.

In an eighteenth-century theatre the final scene would have been similarly elaborate: when David Garrick produced *Romeo and Juliet* in the mid-eighteenth century, the stage had a large set-construction representing the tomb, with tall double doors, erected in front of a backcloth painted to resemble the churchyard — a night sky, trees, moonlight. The first part of the scene took place before the closed tomb; Romeo broke open the doors and entered the tomb to join Juliet. In later theatres this elaborate staging was extended even further: in a nineteenth-century theatre the initial action in the churchyard, and the subsequent action in the tomb, were performed on separate sets, with the curtain drawn to cover the scene-change. When Henry Irving played Romeo at the Lyceum theatre in the 1880s, these two parts of the scene occupied completely different locations: the action before the tomb was played on a churchyard-set, which was removed behind the curtain; and the action within the tomb was performed on another large stage-set, complete with stone walls, vaulted arches, and at the rear of the stage a staircase leading upwards, flooded with moonlight from the churchyard where the previous scene had taken place. Clearly such devices of staging belong to a theatre very different from the bare, unfurnished open space of the Elizabethan stage: but by the time we get to Irving's production, the stage is obviously trying to emulate the theatrical realism later made possible by the medium of film.

Let us consider how differently this 'movement' of the play is constructed in a modern film version, that of Franco Zeffirelli (1968). Film narrative normally operates naturalistically, either by shooting actual locations, or faking them by means of a studio set. *Romeo and Juliet* was filmed over a large number of different locations in Italy, since the director wanted to fill his screen with vivid naturalistic images of Renaissance society and culture. Here is a summary of the film's treatment of these final scenes, taken from Jack Jorgen's *Shakespeare on Film*. The initial number represents a division of the film-text into separate 'scenes', each of which occupies a particular location or studio setting; the number of the filmic 'scene' is followed by the Act and scene division of Shakespeare's text. Most of the filmic 'scenes' have no corresponding Act and scene division, since they have no exact counterpart in Shakespeare's text.

22. (4.3) *Juliet's Room*. Juliet pulls shut the white gauze bed-curtain, drinks the potion.

23. *Outside Friar Laurence's cell. Morning*. Friar Laurence sends a Brother on a donkey with the letter to Romeo.

24. (4.5) *Capulet's house*. Birds sing. Nurse's cry pierces the quiet: 'Juliet is dead!'. The Capulets rush to find it is so.

25. *The Road to Mantua*. The Brother proceeds slowly.

26. (4.5) *Capulet's tomb*. Romeo's man watches Juliet's funeral, rides down tree-lined road.

27. *Road to Mantua*. Romeo's man races past the Brother.

28. *Mantua*. Romeo's man arrives, tells him Juliet is dead.

29. *Road to Verona*. Romeo rides past Brother, through sheep.

30. (5.3) *Verona Churchyard. Night*. Romeo dismisses his man, breaks open the doors of the crypt, passes by rows of rotting corpses to find Juliet. He takes off her shroud, kisses her. Seeing Tybalt's body, he walks to it and

asks his forgiveness. He holds Juliet once again, weeps, drinks poison. The Friar arrives too late. As Juliet wakes he hears the Prince's trumpet, urges her to flee, goes out. She finds Romeo, kisses him, weeps, stabs herself.

31. (5.3) *Verona Square*. Two families united in a funeral procession. Prince angrily: 'All are punished!'. Chorus: 'A glooming peace this morning with it brings./ The sun for sorrow will not show his head./ For never was a story of more woe/ Than this of Juliet and her Romeo'. Members of the two families make gestures of reconciliation, pass by leaving shot of castellated tower and walls of Verona.

The most obvious area of innovation in the film treatment is the addition of scenes depicting pieces of action which in the play-text are narrated or only implied. The plot at this point obviously involves an action spread over space and time, with people moving between one place and another. In a *narrative* medium, all this circumstantial detail would of course be related: Shakespeare's primary source, Arthur Brooke's *The Tragicall Historye of Romeus and Juliet* (1562), a long narrative poem, spends almost 1,000 lines describing these concluding events. But in the *dramatic* text all this narrative detail is severely condensed: we have the Friar's indication that he has a plan, at the end of IV.1, and the arrival of Balthasar in Mantua at the beginning of V.1. Apart from these details, the only scene with a purely narrative function that the play seems to have needed is the brief exchange between Friar Laurence and Friar John in V.2. The film however supplies a running description of the whole plot, by adding six scenes on the road between Verona and Mantua.

It could obviously be argued that the condensed nature of the dramatic text was more a matter of limitation than strength: since the stage could not *show* time or place, dramatists simply had to work around the constraints of their medium. The development of film technology enabled the dramatic arts to occupy those dimensions of space and time that were always at the disposal of the narrative forms such as the epic, the romance and the novel. If Shakespeare had been able, as Zeffirelli was, to deploy a dramatic technology capable of representing the delays and over-hasty dashes that precipitate the tragedy, he would surely, we may feel, have welcomed it. But it is worth remembering that *Romeo and Juliet* was written for the theatre of its time, and worth considering what dramatic potentialities that relationship between dramatist and medium entailed.

Let us return to Juliet's simulated suicide (IV.3), and relocate the action of the play into the performance space of the Elizabethan public theatre. Juliet withdraws and takes her potion in the midst of the busy bustle and preparation of the Capulet household. Act IV scene 2 and scene 4 are simply one continuous action, with Capulet, his lady and the Nurse making their preparations for the wedding feast. As we have seen, when Juliet takes the drug, the stage directions indicate that from this point on in Elizabethan performance, the rest of the play would have been performed continuously, with Juliet never leaving the stage. On drinking the potion *'She falls upon her bed within the curtains'*. Her mother and Nurse enter the stage, though they are not supposed to be in Juliet's bedroom. Capulet and several servants also pass across the stage, while Juliet in her bed remains in full view of the audience. It is only when the Nurse is told to wake her that she moves to the stage-bed, discovers Juliet apparently dead, and calls the attention of the other characters to the girl's silent presence.

The poetic language of the play persistently draws analogies with the maiden's own bed, the wedding bed she should have occupied, and the tomb she occupies in her simulated death. On the Elizabethan stage these were not merely metaphors, since the dramatic action demanded that they be one and the same physical location. When the Friar and Paris enter, they insistently link, in a series of choric laments, love and death, sexual union and dying, the marriage bed and the grave. The obvious parallel between analogous rituals, wedding and funeral, evokes a terrible similarity in the midst of grotesque contrast.

When the characters leave, the stage direction indicates that the Nurse closes the curtain round her bed: which is obviously all the burial Juliet would get on the Elizabethan stage. The tragic atmosphere is then subverted by a comic scene with a group of musicians, whose frivolous joking contrasts sharply with the atmosphere of mourning and bereavement. But then of course (and this is perhaps the point of the interlude) since Juliet is not truly dead, and will soon be reunited with her husband Romeo, the humorous jesting of a wedding feast is perhaps more appropriate to the truth of the situation (i.e. that if all goes according to plan the lovers will shortly be free and reunited) than the sadness of a funeral.

Further analogies between the bed and the grave then appear at the beginning of V.1, as Romeo awaits news of Juliet. He had dreamed that Juliet found him dead, and revived him with a kiss. The vividness of the dream, and its mythical basis in fairy-tale (though normally it is the sleeping maiden who is resurrected by the kiss of a man) convince him that it is an augury of truth. The speech is replete with dramatic ironies: in the event it is Juliet who will wake from apparent death, and her kissing of the dead Romeo, designed to drink up any remaining poison, will be part of her determination to join him in death.

The Elizabethan stage thrived on this dramatic interplay of contradictions: comedy and tragedy, mirth and funeral, love and death, always had to occupy the same physical space, and to coexist in a brief and eventful space of time, 'the two-hours traffic of our stage'. Those developments in theatrical and film technologies which enabled producers and editors to *separate* the different elements, placing them further apart by scene-changes or film editing, may have added a dimension of realism, but may also have detracted from the union of physical and verbal power this particular dramatic text possessed in its original theatrical context of performance.

1

Have subsequent eras been right, in your view, to reinterpret Shakespeare's play in the light of their own theatrical conventions?

2

What freedoms does a film-maker have over a dramatist? Can you see any potential drawbacks to this?

3

What theatrical advantages can you see in staging the close of *Romeo and Juliet* with Juliet's body visible throughout?

4

What significance do you find in the 'analogies between the bed and the grave' (page 28) that Holderness traces in this essay?

Peter Hollindale

Peter Hollindale is Senior Lecturer in English and Education at the University of York. He is General Editor of the Macmillan Shakespeare, and has published numerous books and articles.

The tragic potential of comedy

Romeo and Juliet is authentic tragedy. Yet its position in the canon of Shakespeare's work is anomalous, because it has relatively little in common with the great tragedies of Shakespeare's maturity. Only one of the later tragedies, *Antony and Cleopatra*, will seriously help us in understanding the tragic predicament of *Romeo and Juliet*. The others are potential distractions: they may cause us to discover in *Romeo and Juliet* what is not actually there, or to underrate this early play for failing to display those qualities which the mature tragedies lead us to expect. It is natural enough that we should look for help in understanding any single Shakespeare play by turning to others which in one way or another resemble it, but the closest neighbours of *Romeo and Juliet* are to be found in unexpected places — not amongst the remaining tragedies, but amongst the romantic comedies which Shakespeare was writing at much the same early stage in his career as *Romeo and Juliet*, and amongst the romances which he wrote at the very end of his working life.

For the purposes of argument, tragedy can be divided into two simplistic alternatives: the tragedy of fate, or of fortune, and the tragedy of character. In practice it is very difficult to conceive of any play which could exclusively be termed either one or the other. For example, Sophocles's great tragedy *Oedipus Rex*, which is fundamental to any understanding of tragic form, is ostensibly a tragedy of fate: the catastrophic actions which cause the downfall of Oedipus are committed by him unintentionally, and fulfil a divine edict which was made before his birth; in this sense Oedipus has no responsibility for his fate, but is destroyed by forces which he can neither control nor avoid. On the other hand, the ruinous exposure of what he has done, which has for many years lain innocently hidden from the light, is brought about by his obsessive desire to solve mysteries and riddles and bring truths into the open, and this is a function of character, driving events forward by the force of individual will. Conversely, Shakespeare's *Macbeth* is ostensibly a tragedy of character, precipitated by the irresistible dominance of ambition and desire for power in Macbeth and his wife, but the existence of supernatural forces in the form of the witches (who are also seen and heard by Banquo, and cannot therefore be explained away as personal hallucinations) suggests a concurrent driving force of external fate. Character and fate are interactive presences in most tragic drama, but the bending of a play towards one or other of the alternatives is a (perhaps local and provisional) philosophic bias on the part of the dramatist, reflecting an immediate sense either of humankind's responsibility for its own fate — a kind of psychological causality — or else the lack of such responsibility, if people's tragic downfall is seen to be the outcome of arbitrary fate, fortune, chance or accident.

The habit of modern readers and audiences is to prefer a psychological causality wherever they can find it, and in the great phase of mature Shakespearean tragedy it is easy enough to find. We can even explain much of Shakespearean tragedy, if we so choose, in terms of the Aristotelian 'tragic flaw', the single ruinous fault which destroys an otherwise virtuous and eminent figure: Macbeth is ambitious, Hamlet prevaricates, Othello is jealous, Coriolanus is proud, and so forth. In truth matters are not so simple, and in *Antony and Cleopatra* the complexities are particularly evident. There is no shortage of 'faults' in either Antony or Cleopatra, if we choose to designate them, but that does not alter or discount the fact that the lovers in this play are fatally entrapped between two incompatible worlds. They are, respectively, exalted citizens of Rome and Egypt, and Rome and Egypt are imprisoning social realities which will not let them alone. Their effort to establish for themselves an insulated world of love is doomed by the collision of larger political entities of which they are members whether they like it or not.

Efforts are sometimes made to explain *Romeo and Juliet* as a tragedy of character, and even to discover a 'tragic flaw', which will explain the lovers' fate and make *them* responsible for it. There is evidence to hand if we look for it. The lovers are young and immature; they behave precipitately, in defiance of parental wishes, and secretly, in defiance of parental knowledge. They are, we could say, governed by passion and not by reason, a bias and imbalance which incurred the disapproval of Elizabethan moralists. Romeo, perhaps, is betrayed against his will into violent excess, and fatally subverts his love when he becomes his friend's avenger. Juliet, perhaps, is deceitful when she lies to and misleads her parents, and is irreligious when she uses the pretence of penance and shriving in order to plot further covert disobedience with the Friar. Numerous imperfections are present to reward the diligent searcher, and if they could be summed up in a mutual tragic flaw it would no doubt be 'impetuousness'.

To find assurance that this is *not* how Shakespeare intended us to see and hear his play we need only look to his sources. The story of Romeo and Juliet was well known in the sixteenth century — so popular indeed that we must imagine the play's first audiences in the 1590s as similarly placed to those watching *Julius Caesar* or an English chronicle play. That is to say, they knew the plot and the inevitable outcome. The story first appeared about 1530 in Italy, in Luigi da Porto's *Historia novellamente ritrovata di due nobili amanti*, and not only the general story but the precise sequence of events in it remained unaltered as it made its way through versions and translations across Europe, reaching England in two translations in the 1560s. One of these was that of Arthur Brooke, and what he thought of the story's moral significance is made clear in his Preface (1562):

> ... to this end, good Reader, is this tragical matter written, to

describe unto thee a couple of unfortunate lovers, thralling themselves to unhonest desire; neglecting the authority and advice of parents and friends; conferring their principal counsels with drunken gossips and superstitious friars (the naturally fit instruments of unchastity); attempting all adventures of peril for th'attaining of their wicked lust; using auricular confession, the key of whoredom and treason, for furtherance of their purpose; abusing the honourable name of marriage to cloak the shame of stolen contracts; finally by all means of unhonest life hasting to most unhappy death.

Setting this moralistic diatribe against Shakespeare's treatment of the story, it is apparent at once what pains he took to mitigate the lovers' openness to moral blame. Brooke's complaints are essentially of three kinds: that Romeo and Juliet are guilty of wilful lust; that they are irreligious, especially in prostituting the sacrament of marriage; and that they are unnatural, in flouting family duty and obedience. In Shakespeare, each of these shortcomings is modified to produce a wholly different moral effect. Lust is unmistakably transformed into romantic love, and while it is naturally true that their love embraces physical desire and consummation, it is also true that this youthful rebellion of the flesh against dynastic enmity becomes a private, wholesome reassertion of social health. The sexual union of the lovers is the premature enactment of a social reconciliation that might be. The charge of irreligion is countered by the instantaneousness of their marriage-plan: falling in love and courtship and the recognition of commitment are so telescoped in one transcendent evening that marriage is scarcely even a *consequence* of love: rather it is a natural fusion with the night's romantic miracle, so that love itself takes on (what in the tragic outcome it will eventually become for all Verona) the quality of redemptive sacrament. The charge of unnatural disobedience to parents is subtly discredited by Shakespeare's treatment of old Capulet. When first approached by Paris for Juliet's hand, he initially demurs because she is so young, and then stipulates the need for her own willingness:

My will to her consent is but a part.

(I.2.17)

Yet in III.5 we see him angrily bullying Juliet into precipitate marriage, even within hours of her cousin's death. Old Capulet's intemperance and instability rob him of the paternal authority and dignity which might stigmatise Juliet's secret disobedience.

Clearly, then, *Romeo and Juliet* is not a 'tragedy of character', in which the lovers' moral weakness causes their destruction. On the contrary, Shakespeare has carefully modified his sources to divert responsibility on to external circumstances which the pair cannot control. This is not to say that their own characters play no part in the tragic process, but those very facets of the lovers which propel them to catastrophe — their youth, their challenge to dynastic hatred, their impulsive ardour and sexual delight, their refusal of time's delay — are potentially regenerative qualities, marked out for disaster only because an obsolete quarrel has entrapped them. They are caught between the realities of Montague and Capulet, just as surely as Antony and Cleopatra are caught between Rome and Egypt.

Is this, then, a tragedy of fortune, of fate? Quite clearly it is. The Chorus tells us so at the outset, and reminds the audience of the fatality which the play's first audience already knew. The Chorus's Prologue is a formal sonnet, and uses the sonnet's resources for compact finality of statement. From the first lines of the play we know that the lovers are doomed, and that fortune has so decreed it. They have sprung from the 'fatal' loins of Montague and Capulet, their love is 'star-crossed' and 'death-marked', and their role is predetermined as one of sacrificial social healing. The play declares itself sombre and doom-laden, and is to reinforce that mood throughout by reiterated associations between love and death, and a dazzling poetic concentration of the sudden, the momentary and the intense in love's fulfilment.

Having thus begun in the dark mood to which its ending will be loyal, the play then takes us by surprise. In fact it is a skilful blending of two kinds of play, two genres, and after the fatalistic prelude it proves to have unexpected kinship with romantic comedy. This was, after all, the form in which Shakespeare achieved his earliest phase of mature greatness, and the great comedies are very near to *Romeo and Juliet* in time of composition. *Romeo and Juliet* can helpfully be seen simultaneously in two ways: as a tragedy of fate, and as the great imaginative 'What if . . . ?' of romantic comedy. In mature Shakespearean comedy there is a marked propulsion towards happiness, a climate of imagination in which love achieves eventual fulfilment, and those forces which act against it and obstruct it are finally perceived to be aberrant, and are reconciled or overcome. *Romeo and Juliet* asks the grave 'What if . . . ?' of comedy's logic. What if the wrong turnings are taken, what if the aberration of destructive hatred proves too durable, what if accidents of circumstances are malign and not beneficent, what if the rules are broken? In *Romeo and Juliet*, fate-determined tragedy goes hand in hand with surprising anticipations of comedy, which are raised only to be thwarted. They are dashed by the sterile longevity of the quarrel between Montague and Capulet, and more especially by the actions of Tybalt and Mercutio.

The opening scene at once introduces the comic mode, its tantalising near-security, and the risks to its safe continuance. There is nothing unusual in a tragedy beginning with minor characters or local civic brawls: *Julius Caesar*, for example, begins in this way. But Sampson and Gregory are genuinely funny, and their evident pleasure in bawdy word-play is a spirited emulation of the competitive wit which their social betters trade in. Word-play is their entertainment, as is the quarrel between Montague and Capulet. Our first encounter with dynastic hatred in Verona shows it providing an excuse for servants to have rowdy quarrels in the streets. For the family menials the ancient rancour is a petty, irrational but enticing opportunity for hooligan bravado, a state of affairs which is wholly familiar to us in an age of football riots. As so often in Shakespeare, the opening scene predicts the shape of things to come, and in subsequent scenes of the first half of the play, we see that there is little to choose between Gregory and Sampson and their youthful masters. For the youth of three noble houses, as for their servants, word-play, bawdy repartee and aggressive tribal challenge go together as an entertainment.

The opening scene also shows how easily things can go wrong. Because of the ancient quarrel, Veronese society is highly strung and sensitive, with constant risk that serious violence and civil commotion will issue from accidental eruptions of petty rivalry. The servants are as true as anyone to the temptations of Mercutio's fatal challenge to Tybalt:

> And but one word with one of us? Couple it with something.
> Make it a word and a blow.
>
> (III.1.38–39)

Whatever its dangers, however, this is from the outset a world of comedy, wit, indecent bawdiness and boisterous pleasure which is full of comic potential, and some distance removed from the ominous necessities of fate which marked the opening Chorus sonnet. The effect is reinforced by the signals of attainable order which are current in the opening scenes. The presence of *law*, as a benevolent ordering force in Verona, is felt from the beginning. Gregory and Sampson are anxious to keep 'on the windy side of the law' by not culpably provoking violence: 'Let us take the law of our sides' is their prudent instinct. The outbreak of fighting which overcomes prudence (prophetically ignited by Tybalt's entrance) is subject to well-meant intervention by Benvolio (living up to his good name, as he always does), and only Tybalt frustrates the play's first attempt at intermediary peace-keeping. True order is then restored by the authoritative entrance of the Prince. This pattern of behaviour is an almost exact prediction of the one which will lead in III.1 to irremediable disaster, but this first scene firmly establishes its essential frivolity, its association with verbal sword-play and superficial *macho* gesturing, and its risky defiance of dependable ordering forces.

When old Montague and old Capulet join the brawl, they too do not live up to the impressive advertisement which the Chorus gave them. The 'fatal loins' have been replaced by ageing joints in need of crutches, their 'strife' and 'rage' are turned to superannuated fighting antics from which their wives restrain them. The Prince's speech suggests that what is true of them is true of their supporters: this is not so much a fatal conflict as unseemly mayhem by the ancientry, for reasons they cannot recall. (Shakespeare gives no explanation of the quarrel's origins.) What is announced as portentous is encountered as absurd (with the proviso that absurdities can instigate great harm).

Still more important are the hints that Montague and Capulet are weary of this old antagonism, and would not be averse to letting it rest. Montague asks, 'Who set this ancient quarrel new abroad?' (I.1.104), and Capulet is clearly pleased rather than irritated that the Prince has placed them under mutual constraint:

> But Montague is bound as well as I,
> In penalty alike; and 'tis not hard, I think,
> For men so old as we to keep the peace.
>
> (1.2.1–3)

Significantly, and with clear dramatic irony, both Montague and Capulet are more interested in the futures of their offspring than in the sterile momentum of old antipathies: within minutes of these two speeches, Montague is enquiring into Romeo's lovelorn absences and Capulet negotiating Juliet's marriage. Of all the hints of possible reconciliation, the most pronounced is Capulet's tolerant hospitality to Romeo at the ball, and his fiery denunciation of Tybalt.

Where the feud is concerned, then, all is set up in the opening scenes for a plot of comic complication and eventual resolution. We recognise it as this, even though we know that such an outcome will be denied. Essentially the same is true of romantic love in the play's first phase. Not for nothing does this play speak periodically in sonnets. The convention of love to which we first find Romeo attached is in the post-Petrarchan mode of lovelorn worship, decorated with all the standard hyperboles of Elizabethan sonneteers. In Romeo's eyes, his Rosaline is conventionally matchless; and he himself is devoted to the post-medieval religion of love:

> One fairer than my love? The all-seeing sun
> Ne'er saw her match since first the world begun.
>
> (I.2.91–92)

His cliché-exaggerations of love and ultimate fidelity embrace the romantic commonplaces of the Elizabethan love-sonnet, lamenting Rosaline's proud refusal of his advances and the way this damages the future, depriving it of her beauty's continuance through children:

> O, she is rich in beauty; only poor
> That, when she dies, with beauty dies her store.
>
> (I.1.215–216)

This is wholly appropriate to a world of romantic comedy: in

Twelfth Night Viola makes essentially the same conventional sonneteering plea, poignantly against her own love-interests:

> Lady, you are the cruell'st she alive,
> If you will lead these graces to the grave,
> And leave the world no copy.

In his verbal wit, his punning repartee, his fondness for clever antithesis and paradox, his conventional hyperbole, just as in his taste for melancholic seclusion, his romantic weeping, and his proneness to fickle changes of love-object, the Romeo of the opening scenes is a typical lover in romantic comedy. With similar observations of comic method, the play sets baser, more realistic attitudes against the idealising stereotype: Benvolio advises Romeo to cure his passion by inspecting the full range of available women, advice which old Capulet echoes to Paris; while the Nurse is only the most blatant and garrulous of those for whom love is a merry coarseness of the flesh.

More general features and habitual situations of romantic comedy are typified by these examples. Like the great Shakespearean comedies, *Romeo and Juliet* is a highly social play about a particular, localised society. This society is one where irrational or unexplained malignity is in temporary sway, threatening or overruling a norm of order which is seen as peaceable, benevolent and just. The quarrel of Montagues and Capulets is a more serious aberration than the plotting of Don John in *Much Ado About Nothing*, or the malice of Duke Frederick and Oliver in *As You Like It*, but our sense that it *is* an aberration is just as strong. The arbitrary tyranny of fathers over daughters is another frequent occurrence in comedy: Shakespearean examples include the Duke of Milan in *The Two Gentlemen of Verona* and Egeus in *A Midsummer Night's Dream*. Similarly, the fickleness of male affections and the transformative instancy of love at first sight are major happenings in both these plays.

Arguably the most important single feature of Shakespeare's comic practice which is taken over into *Romeo and Juliet* is the dominance of the heroine. The great names of Shakespearean comedy are those of women: Rosaline in *Love's Labour's Lost*, Viola in *Twelfth Night*, Rosalind in *As You Like It*, Beatrice in *Much Ado*, Portia in *The Merchant of Venice*. Either throughout the play, or in key episodes, these heroines are the leaders, initiators, manipulators and judges of the action. So it is here. Although it is true that Romeo develops markedly in the course of the play, and that the conventions of speech and action described above are utterly outgrown in the few days between Act I and Act V, Juliet is nevertheless the more impressive figure of the two. She takes the initiatives characteristic of the comedy heroine. Although they impel the play towards tragedy, they also express most memorably its great positive of love. As a general rule, Juliet acts whereas Romeo reacts. She it is who fuses love with marriage; she above all is the one who plans and schemes and thinks her way through adverse circumstances; the greatest acts of deliberate courage are hers, as are the two great invocations of love's faith, first in the context of life and consummation (III.2.1–35) and then of death (IV.3.14–59). She is the heroine of comedy transposed to a world of tragic fatedness.

For in all the provisional and delusive comedy of the opening scenes, side by side with the humour and the lyrical sunburst of romantic love run the reminders of the fate first broached by the Chorus, and Juliet as much as Romeo is subject to the shadowy intuition of its presence:

> Although I joy in thee,
> I have no joy of this contract tonight.
> It is too rash, too unadvised, too sudden;
> Too like the lightning, which doth cease to be
> Ere one can say 'It lightens'.
>
> (II.2.116–120)

Just as Romeo does (I.4.106–111), so Juliet perceives the 'Prodigious birth of love' (1.5.140), and it is linked for both of them with thoughts of death.

If we ask where the bounds of comedy are broken, and the wrong turnings taken which convert potential happiness to tragedy, we must look first to the lovers themselves. The dark prodigiousness of their love lies in its very suddenness, and the premature completeness of its being. It is indeed 'too like the lightning', and its clandestine swiftness is too great for it to be attuned with the slow, unsteady atrophy of hatred which seems signified in Montague and Capulet hostility elsewhere. This passion is too youthful, ardent and explosive to perform by its life the Friar's hope that it will 'turn your households' rancour to pure love'. Only by their sacrificial death can Romeo and Juliet do that. It is not because it exists at all, but because it exists with such pace and intensity, that their love is destroyed. Yet the play is an unforgettable celebration of that tragic instancy.

If love breaks the bounds of comedy, so does hate. From the opening scene we are faced with Tybalt as an aberrant, threatening figure. However contemptuously regarded by Mercutio as one who quarrels by the book, Tybalt is also a hot-tempered gangland provocateur, adept at giving the kiss of life to dying enmities. So much is clear, but we are naturally less inclined to point accusing fingers at Mercutio, that delighted and delightful comic spirit. Yet Mercutio, almost as much as Tybalt, is an advocate and beneficiary of Verona's social distemperature — without dynastic rancour but also without dynastic excuse. Between them, they seize the feud and re-invent its deadliness. Mercutio, though of the Prince's house, becomes a surrogate Montague on the streets of Verona, more active and belligerent than either Romeo or Benvolio. In a play which is much concerned with quarrels and interventions, with hostile dualities and third-party mediations, it is Mercutio who precipitates the crisis. Fatally, he and Romeo exchange roles. Mercutio, who should be mediator, becomes a wilful combatant, and Romeo, the prescribed combatant, becomes the mediator. Like Benvolio's before him, his efforts are dashed by Tybalt. It is therefore with the death of Mercutio, its brilliant and misguided comic spirit, that comedy itself disappears from the play. There-after, comedy resurfaces from time to time in ghostly forms — in frantic delusory bereavement which precedes a real one, and in moments of treacherously jocund optimism — but serves only to reaffirm the unstoppable tragic impetus of the drama.

Romeo and Juliet is Shakespeare's only romantic tragedy. If its immediate kinship with the romantic comedies is close, it is closer still in predictive spirit to the late romances. The power of redemptive healing in young love, and its place in reconciling old parental hatreds, can be seen in the loves of Perdita and Florizel in *The Winter's Tale*, and of Miranda and Ferdinand in *The Tempest*. But in the confident, regenerative vision of those plays, the cost is no longer death.

AFTERTHOUGHTS

1

Would you prefer to think of misfortune as arising through external fate or through human error?

2

Does Hollindale convince you that *Romeo and Juliet* is 'not a "tragedy of character"' (page 34)?

3

What links does this essay identify between *Romeo and Juliet* and Shakespeare's comedies?

4

Do you agree with Hollindale's interpretation of Mercutio's role in the play and the significance of his death (page 40)?

John E Cunningham

John E Cunningham currently divides his time between writing and travel. He is the author of numerous critical studies.

ESSAY

The Fourth Man

According to Dryden, Shakespeare complained that he had to kill off Mercutio in the third Act of *Romeo and Juliet* because he was stealing the play: often repeated, this comment is in one way nonsense, for the death is essential to Romeo's killing of Tybalt, and so to the banishment and tragic end; but it makes sense in another way — Mercutio is immensely alive and attractive where his lovelorn friend is not. What is often ignored by those who repeat the observation is that in the central Act no fewer than three of the quartet of young men in this play are dismissed: Mercutio and Tybalt are killed; Benvolio simply vanishes, after being given his only substantial speech, scarcely twenty-five lines of tedious but necessary explanation to the Duke of something which the audience has already seen, the circumstances of the duel and deaths. If the actor who plays the part waits to take a curtain, the audience will almost have forgotten who he was: in Shakespeare's small and hard-working company he probably doubled up as one of the many minor roles in the later part of the play, the worthy Friar John perhaps, who says his few blandly informative lines and passes into a second oblivion.

Yet Shakespeare often takes trouble over quite small roles — his murderers, like his schoolmasters, are a class by themselves — and Benvolio is, I suggest, very much a character in his own right, carefully thought out, as well as someone who makes an important contribution to the action; above all, he is part of a pattern of behaviour of which the original audience would have been well aware, but to which we must learn to attune ourselves. We shall examine these three aspects of his part in order.

If his creator was careful to give his lesser actors something they could get hold of, it was partly because he was an actor himself and understood their difficulties. Early biographers, on scant evidence, assign to him a number of ploddy, secondary parts, of which the Ghost in *Hamlet* and Adam in *As You Like It* are most often cited: less reliably, a stage tradition claims him as Benvolio, who, in his opening appearance, plays the same role of would-be peacemaker in which Adam first appears. There is a pleasant story that his first lines:

> Part, fools!
> Put up your swords. You know not what you do
>
> (I.1.63–64)

originated in an enraged cry from the dramatist because Sampson and Gregory were gagging too much or had got their rehearsed fight wrong, every producer's nightmare. But this, and his opening exchange with Tybalt, set up the character, just as his last lines:

> And to't they go like lightning. For, ere I
> Could draw to part them, was stout Tybalt slain.
> And as he fell, did Romeo turn and fly.
> This is the truth, or let Benvolio die
>
> (III.1.172–175)

sum him up: good-natured, well-meaning, earnest, sincere, reliable — and dull.

After the opening brawl has been silenced, Benvolio gives a perfectly fair account of it to the Montagues and then explains how he has earlier seen Romeo when both men were seeking solitude. His reference to 'a troubled mind' which had sent him into solitude 'pursuing his humour' is about the only suggestion ever made that Benvolio is much disturbed by interior emotions. Clearly the Montagues see him as a solid and reliable friend who will sound out the mystery of their son's behaviour. In the same light he sees himself:

> See, where he comes. So please you step aside.
> I'll know his grievance, or be much denied

(I.1.156–157)

he says, with some self-importance. In the passage which follows he first appears in what is to be an important aspect of his part — that of a butt. Romeo draws elaborate arabesques of paradox about him on the subject of love, leaving him almost speechless. In the end he can offer only obvious advice for hopeless passion, as obvious as it is useless: look at other girls. Pressing his platitudes he scurries offstage after his elusive friend. Evidently he does not have much of a sense of humour, which in itself makes him amusing.

On his next appearance he essays a joke:

> Come, knock and enter; and no sooner in
> Let every man betake him to his legs

(I.4.33–34)

— a sorry play on the possible meanings of 'start to dance' and 'run away' — which is almost immediately followed by one of the most scintillating speeches of the play, Mercutio's fantasy about Queen Mab, at once full of airy wit and bawdy humour about midwives and maids lying on their backs. In such company Benvolio does not shine, but he seems perfectly happy to go along to the party and enjoy himself in his stolid way.

When he and Mercutio return, their friend having given them the slip, he shows another aspect of his nature, or at least suggests it: he is, unusually in young men, rather strait-laced. In this passage (II.1) Mercutio indulges in a series of splendid improprieties about Rosaline's quivering thighs, and the sexually shaped fruits of the medlar and the poppering pear: Benvolio says gravely that Romeo will be annoyed if he hears him talking like that. The same near-prudery is exhibited in II.4, when Mercutio and the newly inspired Romeo are swapping amazing puns. Mercutio embarks on a highly improper image of an idiot running about exposing himself — 'Stop there!' cries the respectable member of the party, only to provoke an even grosser joke.

In the last scene in which he appears — the first of Act III — he is described in affectionate irony by his friend. Having — typically — begun the scene as a peacemaker:

> I pray thee, good Mercutio, let's retire.
> The day is hot, the Capels are abroad.
> And if we meet we shall not 'scape a brawl,
> For now, these hot days, is the mad blood stirring.
>
> (III.1.1–4)

— excellent advice in view of what follows — he is treated to a description of himself as the most fearful picker of quarrels. This tells us two things about him, perhaps three: that he is in fact most reluctant to do any such thing, the very opposite of Tybalt and Mercutio himself; that he does not in the least mind being rallied in this way; and, surely, that Mercutio is fond of him to tease him so for a failing he does not have. A few moments later it is Benvolio's reliable arm that helps the stricken Mercutio to a place for him to die in, Benvolio's simple grief that tells us of his passing, Benvolio's sturdy sense that urges the dazed Romeo to flight, and Benvolio who gives a scrupulous account to the Duke of what has happened, before he leaves the stage himself for good.

If somewhat negative, the character is well drawn, actable. We have also seen that Benvolio has quite a significant part to play in the action, though in a simple synopsis of the work his name commonly passes unmentioned. He plays the peacemaker in a play about a feud, the voice of reason where everyone else but the Duke is swayed by passion or faction. He serves as a reporter. Perhaps most important, and easily missed, he serves as a foil to the play's wit. This has already been suggested in discussing the scenes en route for and after the ball: it is at its most important in II.4, where Romeo and Mercutio embark on one of those dazzling exchanges of punning conceits in which the Elizabethans delighted and which we, even when we can follow them, find so tediously precious. When Mercutio runs off a series of jokes about lovers and ends by asking, 'And is he [Romeo] a man to encounter Tybalt?', Benvolio, who has apparently never been taught that rhetorical questions should remain un-answered, replies by a query about Tybalt, so prompting Mercutio to the 'Prince of Cats' fantasy, based on an extravagant, bilingual pun. When Romeo arrives, the word-play falls about them like confetti, until Mercutio cries:

> Come between us, good Benvolio! My wit faints.
>
> (II.4.66–67)

Benvolio has been taking no part in these gasconades — his wits are not up to it, it is contrary to his nature — but he has been the sole audience onstage; and his responses — whether delighted laughter or more probably extreme perplexity at what he cannot quite follow — will help the audience that actually is out there in the theatre to enjoy what is rather a recondite exercise in amusement. Since many of Shakespeare's original spectators would have had difficulty in following such extreme flights of wit, this function must have been as important when he wrote as it is now, when changes of language and fashions in humour have made it harder than ever to earn laughs in such a scene.

We have just used the word 'humour' in its modern sense, as we have several times used the word 'character': it is time to ask what Shakespeare meant by these terms — what Hamlet was talking about when he said, of the company of strolling players, 'the humorous man shall end his part in peace'. Editors usually say that 'the humorous man' was a character actor — but this itself is to use the word 'character' in an otherwise outmoded way, to mean someone who exhibits a single trait, jealousy or ill-temper for example, to a highly exaggerated, perhaps amusing degree. 'Character', as we have been using it, means a complex of psychological tendencies, some genetic, some acquired through social and other conditioning, to produce a type which we can roughly classify for convenience in discussion.

Shakespeare, in a tradition two thousand years old when he wrote, thought that our characters fell into four groups, according to the 'humour', the bodily fluids of choler, blood, black bile and phlegm, which happened to prevail in our physical make-up: hence men — he uses the system less positively of women — were choleric, sanguine, melancholy or phlegmatic, or some mixture, some 'complexion', of these. Once this system of thought is grasped — the fact that we still use some of its vocabulary suggests that it is not without meaning for us, however insecure its physiological and medical basis propounded by Hippocrates — it is easy to see that in *Romeo and Juliet* he had the idea, which he was to develop to even greater effect later, of presenting and contrasting four men of approximately the same age and rank who represented exactly these four 'humours'.

Each is established as soon as he makes his entrance. Tybalt bounds on to the stage ready to eat Benvolio for breakfast, spoiling for combat, with no thought of a reason:

> What, art thou drawn among these heartless hinds?
> Turn thee, Benvolio, look upon thy death.

(I.1.65–66)

He is the choleric man — a trait he shares with his father, hence the spat between them during the ball, when old Capulet shows he can be as fiercely abrupt as his son. Mercutio we first meet on his way to that same ball, bluff, hearty and extrovert:

> If love be rough with you, be rough with love.
> Prick love for pricking, and you beat love down.
> Give me a case to put my visage in.
> A visor for a visor! What care I
> What curious eye doth quote deformities?
> Here are the beetle brows shall blush for me.

(I.4.27–32)

This is the sanguine man at his best and most likeable. Romeo, as we learn before we even see him, is a solitary, weary of life:

> Towards him I made. But he was ware of me
> And stole into the covert of the wood.

(I.1.124–125)

He is so unhappy that he wishes the day were more advanced than it is: 'Is the day so young?' he asks when he is given a 'Good morrow' at his first entrance. He is melancholy, a type which in the extreme is what we should now call a depressive, prone to despair, potentially suicidal.

Benvolio, whose first words as we have seen are an attempt to still the passions of others, whose last speech tries to give a collected account of a bloody fray in which he has lost his best friends — one to death, the other to flight and exile — makes up the quartet: the phlegmatic.

It would be easy to suppose that Shakespeare, merely for the sake of an arbitrary symmetry, threw off this last and slightest character to complement the other, more interesting, humours. Phlegmatic people are not, by definition, very lively, and do not lend themselves to 'dramatic' situations because they are always under control: at worst rather stolid, even lumpish.

Yet, just as the humours themselves consist of a set of antithetical properties, so characters endowed with them can be played off against each other with effect.

In the elaborate cosmography of the ancients, which Shakespeare inherited and used for his own purposes — 'Does not our lives consist of the four elements?' asks Sir Toby in *Twelfth Night* (II.3.9) — the four elements of which everything was made, earth, air, fire and water with their attendant properties of cold, dryness, heat and moisture, were associated with the four humours: thus blood and choler were both hot, melancholy and phlegm were cold. When two 'hot' characters meet, the fur will fly. The brawl and fight at the beginning of Act III, between Tybalt and Mercutio, perfectly illustrates this: these two men were born to be abrasive to each other. The 'cold' character of Romeo is always at a disadvantage with Tybalt, though when he is roused to revenge, against his own nature, by the foul death of his friend, he is deadly indeed. One suspects, from the description of her, that the unseen Rosaline was of a hotter temperament than her forlorn swain, which was perhaps the attraction for him.

But when Benvolio and Romeo, two 'cold' temperaments, are together, nothing much happens: Benvolio, as we have seen, offers his friend dull, good advice and is mildly mocked. Introduce another 'element', however, and the value of having a phlegmatic man in the quartet is apparent. Mercutio strikes sparks off their solemn friend, and encourages Romeo — now emboldened by his love for Juliet — to do the same in the battle of puns that we have already discussed. Similarly, at the beginning of Act III, when Benvolio, true to his nature, has urged retirement for the sake of peace, a lot of the fun arises from the fact that, when he says he is describing Benvolio, Mercutio actually describes his exact opposite, a choleric man — a Tybalt, in fact:

> Nay, an there were two such, we should have none shortly, for one would kill the other. Thou! Why, thou wilt quarrel with a man that hath a hair more or a hair less in his beard than thou hast. Thou wilt quarrel with a man for cracking nuts, having no other reason but because thou hast hazel eyes.
>
> (III.1.15–20)

In the same way, the force of Mercutio's brief epitaph:

> O Romeo, Romeo, brave Mercutio's dead!
> That gallant spirit hath aspired the clouds,
> Which too untimely here did scorn the earth

(III.1.116–118)

is enhanced because the speaker usually keeps his emotions on a tight rein.

Benvolio, then, is much more than a mere stolid lump, though his lumpishness, in contrast with his livelier companions, can amuse, and in some productions he is remorselessly played for laughs, surely a distortion of the balance Shakespeare had in mind. In seeking to achieve such a balance, however, the playwright was in something of a dilemma: the 'hot' characters are always going to be more dramatically effective, in an immediate way, than the 'cold' ones; though the melancholy man is probably more psychologically interesting because he is, by definition, introspective, self-analytical, in a way that none of the others are supposed to be.

So, when Dryden said that Shakespeare claimed he had to kill Mercutio off, he was probably referring to this surface attraction that the character has — though Dryden himself said he thought the comment unsound. Shakespeare surely had greater problems with his Fourth Man. The fiery Tybalt and the bold, outgoing Mercutio are gifts to a pair of strong actors; Romeo is an interesting romantic lead; but poor old-young Benvolio?

Yet the difficulties of the phlegmatic character in an effective drama have been, as we have seen, well met; and the part is of further interest in that here may be seen a sketch for more ambitious explorations of this humour.

It was to be examined in its noblest aspect in the Stoic, Brutus, who is, for many, a character more impressive than Julius Caesar himself: but the role of the phlegmatic friend is surely presented at its most touching in a slightly later tragedy, in which, as in *Romeo and Juliet*, four men of approximately similar age and aristocratic standing are played off against one another according to their humours.

So, in *Hamlet*, it is still the melancholic who leads; the sanguine man, Fortinbras, has only a tiny if significant part, sometimes cut, to the great loss of the play; the choleric youth, Laertes, is used again as an instrument of revenge in a duel, and is better developed than Tybalt; but Horatio, the phlegmatic friend, represents this humour at its most affecting, and Shakespeare describes the type for all time with an admiration approaching envy:

> And blessed are those
> Whose blood and judgement are so well commeddled
> That they are not a pipe for Fortune's finger
> To sound what stop she please. Give me that man
> That is not passion's slave, and I will wear him
> In my heart's core, ay, in my heart of heart,
> As I do thee.

(III.2.78–84)

While no aspiring actor ever began a brilliant career by playing Benvolio — believe me — there is more to his role and his character than a mere Fourth Gentleman whose name translates as 'Well-meaning'.

AFTERTHOUGHTS

1

Can you think of any 'good-natured, well-meaning, earnest, sincere, reliable' Shakespearean characters who *aren't* also 'dull' (page 43)?

2

Do you agree that the play's wit is difficult to stage successfully (pages 45–46)?

3

Explain the significance of the theory of the 'humours' (page 46) to Cunningham's analysis of the quartet of characters under discussion. How convinced are you by this analysis?

4

Do you see any other links between *Hamlet* and *Romeo and Juliet*, apart from those cited at the close of this essay?

Michael Spiller

Michael Spiller teaches in the English Department at the University of Aberdeen, and is the author of numerous critical studies.

ESSAY

The 'yoke of stars': power and compulsion

It is under the stars that Romeo and Juliet enter the play, as the Prologue announces, 'A pair of star-crossed lovers', and it is under the stars that they leave it, as Romeo, about to take the poison, determines to shake off 'the yoke of inauspicious stars'. Yet whatever sense of things destined and unavoidable there may be in these images, most readers and watchers of the play have a very strong feeling that this is a tragedy of pure chance — or mischance, if you will — which by the merest alteration of a moment could have turned into a comedy. For Romeo dies, let us remind ourselves, because of two separate chance occurrences: first, Friar Laurence's letter, which should have warned Romeo of Juliet's stratagem, is held up in Mantua because of a sudden quarantine imposed upon its bearer, Friar John (V.2); and secondly, Juliet fails to wake before Romeo drinks the fatal liquid. No human malice causes either of these mischances.

Before we examine in detail the great speech (V.3.74–120) in which Romeo confronts his fate before he dies, we must think a little about the problem of chance in tragedy. In real life, people do die, or suffer greatly, because of chance events, and it might be said that what happens to Romeo and Juliet is simply an imitation of what we are unfortunately (I use the word deliberately) familiar with in life. To help us, however, to think more clearly about tragedy both in life and in literature, it is useful to distinguish between *how* something happens and *why* it happens. 'How' refers to the mechanism of events that brings the thing to pass: if a child dies of meningitis, we can trace a viral infection in the body to the point where life ceases — we know *how* it happens. But to ask 'Why?' is to pose a question of a different kind: it is to suppose that there is, or that there should be, some power in the universe which can make the child live or die, and then to ask about its purposes. Unless we are religious, we are very uncertain that such a power exists; if we are securely religious, we have usually been taught that His purposes are unknowable. In either case, the question 'Why?' cannot often in life receive a satisfactory answer.

But in fiction, whether in drama or in the novel, tragedy is crucially different. *Chance does not exist in fiction*, for there is always an author, whose decision it has been to make such and such a 'chance event' take place. In *Romeo and Juliet*, it is Shakespeare's decision to make Friar John be fatally delayed in Mantua, and to make Juliet remain asleep until Romeo has drunk his potion and is dead — to those who inhabit the world of the play, this may look like chance; but we inhabit the world of the author, and we know better. And even if an author is uncertain why a thing was made to happen, or even chooses to be evasive about it, we can still be certain that the thing was done deliberately, and we can ask (though we may not be answered), 'Why did you make it happen *this* way, and not *that*?'

One further general point needs to be made before we turn to the text of *Romeo and Juliet*. Just as fiction differs from life in the respect that there is no chance in fiction, so, within fiction, drama differs from the novel (in prose or in verse) in the way 'chance' can be explained. Formally, most novels have a narrator, a voice speaking in it over the heads of the characters, a voice which can explain the author's purpose to the reader. In Hardy's *Tess of the d'Urbervilles*, a voice is heard at the close of the novel explaining, though very cryptically, the mischances which have befallen the heroine: 'The President of the Immortals, in Aeschylean phrase, had finished his sport with Tess.' In drama, there is no such voice, no one to explain the author's choice. Of course, the author may invent a voice, like the Common Man in

Robert Bolt's *A Man for All Seasons*, who seems to have a privileged relationship with the audience; or he may use a Prologue (as in *Romeo and Juliet*) or an Epilogue (as in *The Tempest*) to create a voice that is not exactly in the play nor yet out of it; and when that happens, we have a sense of a hot line to the author being switched on. Yet Shakespeare himself created a Prologue in *Troilus and Cressida* which explicitly warns us that he is not 'in confidence/ Of author's pen or actor's voice'; and we ought to be cautious about accepting what any Prologue or Epilogue says as coming straight from the author with hand on heart.

In 'interrogating Shakespeare' as to what he meant by making things happen by 'chance' in *Romeo and Juliet*, we have a curious kind of negative evidence available to us, because we know where he got the story, and we can see what he chose not to do with it. Shakespeare was all his life very reluctant to invent plots, and the story of Romeo and Juliet, which was a well-known tale in his day, was supplied to him by Arthur Brooke's verse-novel *The Tragicall Historye of Romeus and Juliet*, published in 1562.[1] Brooke gives Shakespeare all his material except for the character of Mercutio (the name occurs in Brooke, but not the figure that Shakespeare draws); and frequently suggests the outline and even the imagery of a speech — Juliet's 'charnel house' speech (IV.3.15–58) is very closely adapted from forty lines of Brooke. But Shakespeare did not borrow inertly or lazily: one short example here must stand for many to show how thoughtfully he handled what was in front of him.

In Romeo's final speech (V.3.74–120), there occurs what might seem a bizarre interruption in his impassioned farewell to Juliet: in the midst of the marvellous metaphor of Death the Conqueror, Romeo suddenly notices Tybalt's corpse:

> [To Juliet] Thou art not conquered. Beauty's ensign yet
> Is crimson in thy lips and in thy cheeks,
> And death's pale flag is not advancèd there.

---

[1] If you would like to read Brooke's version of the story to see what Shakespeare had in front of him as he wrote, it is reprinted in the Arden edition of the play, edited by Brian Gibbons (London, 1980), Appendix II.

Tybalt, liest thou there in thy bloody sheet?

(V.3.94–97)

The shift of attention is suggested by Brooke, and Shakespeare follows obediently; but after the words addressed to Tybalt, Brooke as it were offered Shakespeare a perfectly sensible next move, which he declined: Romeus in Brooke's narrative moves into a speech of religious repentance, and then dies. Shakespeare, brilliantly and movingly, makes Romeo notice again how warm Juliet's flesh still seems by immediate contrast with Tybalt's; and with a telling stress on the word 'thou' he embarks upon another great metaphor of the power of Death — Brooke's conventional religiosity is quite ignored:

> [To Tybalt] Forgive me, cousin! Ah, dear Juliet,
> Why art thou yet so fair? Shall I believe
> That unsubstantial death is amorous,
> And that the lean abhorrèd monster keeps
> Thee here in dark to be his paramour?

[V.3.101–105)

Instances such as this justify our saying that when Shakespeare diverged from his source, he had his own purposes; when he followed it, he was being offered exactly what he wanted. In looking, then, at Romeo's great death speech for evidence of Shakespeare's 'Why?' (the *how* is clear enough in all the swiftly plotted comings and goings in and around the tomb), we may note three interesting departures from Brooke's narrative. First, Shakespeare substitutes a quick-acting poison for a slow-acting one in Brooke: Romeus takes the poison and then speaks, Romeo speaks and then takes it. Second, Shakespeare gives Juliet almost nothing to say before dying: she is hurried into stabbing herself by the arrival of the Watch (V.3.169), whereas Brooke allows her fifty lines of affecting lament. And lastly, reversing that emphasis, Shakespeare extends the ten lines which Brooke allows to Romeus into thirty-five (if we ignore for the moment that part of the speech concerned with Paris, who does not appear in Brooke at this point).

Taking these facts in the direction in which they seem to point, let us suggest this: Shakespeare would not have declined a very affecting death speech from Juliet — a compelling piece of theatre and one which his boy-actor was obviously capable of handling, given the rest of the part — nor would he have ignored Brooke's material and written a very long speech of his own for Romeo, unless that speech contained something of crucial importance, something moreover which he could not allow to be upstaged by anything Juliet might say. (In passing, the history of the production of *Romeo and Juliet* from the late-seventeenth to mid-eighteenth century reminds us that there was another infinitely touching possibility which, since it occurred to Otway and to Garrick,[2] Shakespeare must surely have seen but resisted: that Juliet wakes *after* Romeo takes the poison but *before* he dies, thus providing a heartbreaking duet. If Shakespeare saw this, he banished it sternly from his mind.) Now, the thing that seems to be so important as to warrant this sacrifice of a splendid *coup de théâtre* was first noticed at the end of the eighteenth century by a critic named Whiter, who drew attention, without knowing quite what to make of it, to a 'strange coincidence' involving the lines in which the 'yoke of stars' is mentioned:

> Here, here will I remain
> With worms that are thy chambermaids. O here
> Will I set up my everlasting rest
> And shake the yoke of inauspicious stars
> From this world-wearied flesh. Eyes, look your last!
> Arms, take your last embrace! and, lips, O you
> The doors of breath, seal with a righteous kiss
> A dateless bargain to engrossing death!
> Come, bitter conduct, come, unsavoury guide!
> Thou desperate pilot, now at once run on
> The dashing rocks thy seasick weary bark!
> Here's to my love! (*He drinks*) O true Apothecary!
> Thy drugs are quick. Thus with a kiss I die.

(V.3.108–120)

Whiter saw that these lines are strongly reminiscent of

---

[2] For this and other interesting facts about the production history of the play, see Jill L Levenson, *Romeo and Juliet*, Shakespeare in Performance series (Manchester, 1987).

Romeo's earlier speech of presentiment before he and his friends enter Capulet's house to gatecrash the feast:

> . . . my mind misgives
> Some consequence, yet hanging in the stars,
> Shall bitterly begin his fearful date
> With this night's revels and expire the term
> Of a despisèd life, closed in my breast,
> By some vile forfeit of untimely death.
> But He that hath the steerage of my course
> Direct my sail!
>
> (I.4.106–113)

'The curious reader', says Whiter, 'will not fail to observe that the ideas drawn from the Stars, the Law and the Sea succeed each other in both speeches, in the same order, though with a different application.'[3] Indeed they do, and at the cost of considerable implausibility, for there is no reason at all why Romeo before the Capulets' feast should suddenly think these thoughts: he is heavy of heart because he is lovesick for Rosaline at this point, not because he is feeling 'despised'. 'A rather clumsy speech,' Nicholas Brooke calls it in his account of the play,[4] and psychologically it is; but unless Shakespeare was simply so fatigued when writing *Romeo and Juliet* that he didn't notice that he was repeating himself, we have here what critics call a *motif*: an image or image-cluster that recurs throughout a work to keep certain ideas or concepts present to the reader or audience. Characters who employ motif imagery may not know that they are doing so: Romeo, when he speaks of the stars here in Act I, does not know that he will speak of them again in Act V, nor does he know that he has been described as a 'star-crossed lover' in the Prologue. The motif, and its significance, come from the author to the reader through the characters, and can thus be taken as evidence of the author's preoccupations, especially when, as here, he seems to have taken special pains to include it. Then too, if we find the motif in other works by the same

---

[3] Quoted in the New Variorum edition of the play, edited by H H Furness (New York, 1871; reprinted by Dover Books, New York, 1963), pp. 282–283.
[4] Nicholas Brooke, *Shakespeare's Early Tragedies* (London, 1968), p. 94.

author, we may take it as evidence of a habitual preoccupation, or mental set, of that author — a point to which I shall return later.

The three images that occur in both speeches are all concerned with power, with the powers that control human life, or are felt to do so. These powers are: first, the stars, which hold men's fates suspended over them, a 'consequence hanging' or a 'yoke'; second, Death, with whom human beings sign a dated contract whose 'term' Death can cause to 'expire' by 'forfeit', and who, when they die, 'engrosses' (that is, 'fills out') a new contract, with no date, since there is no release from death; and third, 'he that hath the steerage', the 'pilot' of the human ship through the sea of life. Shakespeare does not allow Romeo to explain whom or what he means by this steersman or pilot: in the former speech, the sentence 'But he that hath the steerage of my course/ Direct my sail' (I.4.112–113)[5] may simply mean 'If any power is controlling my destiny, then let it tell me what to do next'; in

---

[5] This line provides a neat example of the power of editors to affect Shakespeare's meaning by very tiny changes of punctuation and spelling. The Penguin edition, used throughout the present volume, puts a capital at 'he', thus making Romeo appear at this point, as the Penguin Introduction says (pp. 22–23 and note) to be putting his trust in God. But this capital is not there in the texts of the play published in Shakespeare's age, since his printers used small letters even for the divine pronouns; and at this moment Romeo, who is very much the Petrarchan lover, is much more likely to be thinking of Cupid, God of Love. Further, the Penguin editor does not warn the reader that there is a choice of readings later in this line: one of the texts published in Shakespeare's age, the Folio, gives us:

> But he that hath the stirrage of my course,
> Direct my sute

and the other, the first Quarto, has what the Penguin editor chooses:

> But he that hath the steerage of my course
> Direct my saile.

If the word is 'sute' (i.e. 'suit') then Romeo is clearly thinking of his suit to Rosaline, and 'he' must be Cupid; if the word is 'saile', then Romeo is thinking more generally of his future fortunes, and 'he' may indeed be God or Providence, but may also be Cupid, or whatever power rules the affairs of men. As we do not have Shakespeare's manuscript to decide the matter, editors must choose. My argument in this essay obviously depends upon this doubtfulness in the text.

the latter speech, the 'desperate pilot' is the human will (often represented as the steersman of the psychic ship), which here (V.3.117) is Romeo's resolve to drink the poison, his 'bitter conduct'. If at first reading it is a little difficult to see what Romeo is referring to here, notice how skilfully Shakespeare makes Romeo 'internalise' the poison as he prepares to drink it: it moves from being an external bitter liquid ('Come, bitter conduct') to something at one with his own self ('Thou desperate pilot') through a bridging metaphor ('unsavoury guide'). If we leave out of this the Christian scheme of providence and redemption (and you will recall that Shakespeare cut out of his death scene the speech of religious contrition which Arthur Brooke supplied), then these powers together constitute a kind of metaphysics of life, an answer to the 'Why?' that lies beyond the physical 'How?' Not just for Shakespeare, but for the age in which he lived, human life could appear as a kind of arena — theatre, law court, games board; the metaphors are numerous — in which human beings by exercise of their wills made certain moves against Time and Death, choosing freely though always within a set of rules; and above or outside this arena were the judges/spectators: the gods, the stars, the fates — who had power over the whole arena and would sometimes intervene, but often simply let the power struggle continue to its 'term'. Shakespeare, who had himself often stood on a stage before spectators, depending on their applause, condensed the idea into one sombre image in Sonnet 15:

> ... this huge stage presenteth naught but shows
> Whereon the stars in secret influence comment

> (lines 3—4)

Here, in the course of our interrogation of Shakespeare, we can go outside *Romeo and Juliet* to a work whose voice, or voices, is certainly more closely related to Shakespeare than is Romeo's: critics agree that *Romeo and Juliet* was written in the mid-1590s, probably in 1595, and that at the same time Shakespeare was writing his sonnets — circulating among friends, but not to be published until 1609. Now *Romeo and Juliet* has complete sonnets in it, and is full of the rhetoric of contemporary love sonnets, so much so that one critic suggests that 'the play can partly be seen as a dramatic exploration of the world of the love sonnet'.[6] But the world of Shakespeare's love sonnets is not the simple love-sick solitude that Montague describes (I.1.131–142), nor the innocent dance of the encountering lovers (I.5.93–110), but a darker and more bitter universe, in which an older man loves a younger, and rages against the powers of fortune, which separate them by reason of rank, and of time and death, which will separate them by his ageing.

The domination of the world of nature and natural human relations by the grimmer powers is marked in the *Sonnets* by what one might call metaphorical invasion: metaphors from law and from physical decay encroach on human growth, as in the famous Sonnet 18, in which, we note, images from the heavens, the law and the sea appear, with the image of Death the conqueror:

> Shall I compare thee to a summer's day?
> Thou art more lovely and more temperate:
> Rough winds do shake the darling buds of May,
> And summer's lease hath all too short a date. [law]
> Sometime too hot the eye of heaven shines,
> And often is his gold complexion dimm'd;   [the heavens]
> So every fair from fair sometime declines,
> By chance or nature's changing course
>   untrimm'd;   [the sea]
> But thy eternal summer shall not fade,
> Nor lose possession of that fair thou ow'st   [law]
> Nor shall Death brag thou wanderest in his shade,
> When in eternal lines to time thou grow'st:
> > So long as men can breathe, or eyes can see,
> > So long lives this, and this gives life to thee.

This is not the place to talk about the complicated emotions of the *Sonnets*, further than to suggest, as I have been doing, that these perceptions, these feelings or intuitions about the way human love is governed were in Shakespeare's head and in his recurring metaphors at the time he wrote *Romeo and Juliet*, and drove him to make the alterations we have noticed in this essay. Certainly, he is well aware of the volcanic power of sexual desire

---

[6] Nicholas Brooke, *Shakespeare's Early Tragedies*, (London, 1968), p. 80.

in an adolescent girl, and allows Juliet to express it with wonderful directness (III.2.1–31); but he will not have her feminine force compete with Romeo at the end — her last, powerful image, uniting sexual intercourse and death, is only an iteration of what Romeo has already said about Death the Lover:

> ROMEO   Shall I believe
> That unsubstantial death is amorous,
> And that the lean abhorrèd monster keeps
> Thee here in dark to be his paramour?
>
> (V.3.102–105)

> JULIET   Then I'll be brief. O happy dagger!
> This is thy sheath; there rust, and let me die.
>
> (V.3.169–170)

No, the end of the play is Romeo's, and it is Romeo's without any Christian consolation or repentance. However implausible it is that an adolescent should think thus, his creator will have him voice here Shakespeare's troubled and bitter sense that, as he makes another young lover suddenly say in *A Midsummer Night's Dream*, 'quick bright things come to confusion' — not for anything they have done or caused or willed, but because:

> . . . everything that grows
> Holds in perfection but a little moment,
> That this huge stage presenteth naught but shows,
> Whereon the stars in secret influence comment
>
> (Sonnet 15, lines 1–4)

and it is in obedience, all unknowing, to the metaphysics of his author-god that Romeo resolves to end his show, and be no longer subject to the whispering stars.

AFTERTHOUGHTS

1

Do you agree with Spiller's argument that *'Chance does not exist in fiction'* (page 53)?

2

Summarise Spiller's view of the significance of the changes Shakespeare made to his source material.

3

How important, in your opinion, are the links suggested in this essay between *Romeo and Juliet* and Shakespeare's sonnets?

4

'No, the end of the play is Romeo's' (page 61). Do you agree? And, if so, does this make Romeo a more important character than Juliet?

Michael Mangan

Michael Mangan lectures in English at Sheffield University, and is the author of numerous critical studies.

ESSAY

'Whining poetry': *Romeo and Juliet* and love poetry

> *I am two fools, I know,*
> *For loving, and for saying so*
> *In whining poetry.*

(John Donne, 'The Triple Fool')

Romeo, of course, first appears in the play as a joke, as an Elizabethan stereotype. He is the Young Man in Love, the 'Petrarchan' lover of the sonnet sequences which were the stock-in-trade of the Elizabethan courtly poet. Sighing with unrequited passion, pining for a cruel lady who despises his love, he loiters alone in sycamore groves, shunning friends and family. His father describes the way he has been acting:

> Many a morning hath he there been seen
> With tears augmenting the fresh morning's dew,
> Adding to clouds more clouds with his deep sighs.
> But all so soon as the all-cheering sun
> Should in the farthest East begin to draw
> The shady curtains from Aurora's bed,

Away from light steals home my heavy son
And private in his chamber pens himself,
Shuts up his windows, locks fair daylight out,
And makes himself an artificial night.

(I.1.131–140)

Tears, clouds, sighs and night: these are the images which are initially associated with Romeo — and with which he associates himself. Other characters' descriptions of him are borne out when the audience first encounters him. He makes his entrance onto a stage which, a moment or two before had been bristling with action. From the speed and energy of the opening moments, the play shifts down several gears as Romeo tells Benvolio about his melancholy. Throughout this early conversation Romeo speaks the language of the Petrarchan lover, a language stuffed with bad poetry, paradoxes, doleful conceits and self-pitying wit. Even the scene of the recent street fight serves only to fuel his melancholic muse:

Here's much to-do with hate, but more with love.
Why then, O brawling love, O loving hate,
O anything, of nothing first create!
O heavy lightness, serious vanity,
Misshapen chaos of well-seeming forms,
Feather of lead, bright smoke, cold fire, sick health,
Still-waking sleep, that is not what it is!
This love feel I, that feel no love in this.
Dost thou not laugh?

(I.1.175–183)

And yes — of course Benvolio is laughing, though he denies the fact: he is laughing at this farrago of borrowed metaphors and second-hand oxymorons which Romeo is uttering. Moreover, not content with stale images and melodramatic apostrophes, Romeo then breaks into rhymed couplets in a clichéd tribute to his lady's beauty and cruelty:

She'll not be hit
With Cupid's arrow. She hath Dian's wit,
And, in strong proof of chastity well armed,
From love's weak childish bow she lives uncharmed.
She will not stay the siege of loving terms,

Nor bide th'encounter of assailing eyes,
Nor ope her lap to saint-seducing gold.
O, she is rich in beauty; only poor
That, when she dies, with beauty dies her store.

(I.1.208–216)

These last lines might alert us — if we have not already been alerted — to something important that is going on here. Romeo is the lover-as-poet, displacing desire into verse. It is worth remembering that Shakespeare himself was an adept writer of love poetry. Indeed, the sonnet sequence which Shakespeare wrote at about the same time as *Romeo and Juliet* stands as one of the great collections of erotic poetry in English literature. Moreover, a central theme of the first seventeen sonnets of that sequence (which, just to complicate matters, are addressed to a man) is the idea that a person of great physical beauty has a duty not to live chaste, but to have children so that their beauty should not be lost to the world in future generations: precisely what Romeo says about his lady in the lines quoted above. Romeo's love poetry bears at least a passing relationship to Shakespeare's own. It is as if Shakespeare, in one of his moments of mild self-parody, were creating a hero out of a sonnet sequence, a protagonist whose emotional life is constructed by the thoughts, words and emotions of a literary genre, and who *lives* the experience of being a Petrarchan lover. The sonnet sequence is a particularly self-conscious literary genre, one that frequently delights in its own artificiality. The transfer of this kind of rhetoric to the spoken word of the stage, with its claims to imitate everyday speech, inevitably leaves its speaker looking a little foolish; and this is precisely the case with Romeo in the early parts of the play.

We are not told, during this conversation between Romeo and Benvolio, who the object of Romeo's adoration is. We may well — given the title of the play — assume that the cruel beauty about whom he is talking is Juliet. It is not until the following scene that we discover that the key relationship in the play's opening scenes is not 'Romeo and Juliet' but 'Romeo and Rosaline'. And just as the sonneteer's loved one is so often addressed in her absence, so Rosaline, Romeo's disdainful lady, never actually appears in the play. For it is this courtly-love relationship which Romeo will transcend during the play. The love affair which he embarks on in Act I scene 5 takes him beyond the scenario which he initially understands as 'being in love'. And as he outgrows the old conventions, so his language changes: as he develops as a character, he also progresses through a series of ways of using language.

Not immediately, of course. Learned responses are not so easily shrugged off, and Romeo's first instinct on seeing Juliet across a crowded room at the Capulet's ball, is to break once more into rhyme.

> O, she doth teach the torches to burn bright!
> It seems she hangs upon the cheek of night
> As a rich jewel in an Ethiop's ear —
> Beauty too rich for use, for earth too dear!
> . . .
> Did my heart love till now? Forswear it, sight!
> For I ne'er saw true beauty till this night.
>
> (I.5.44–47, 52–53)

Romeo and Juliet, of course, was the source of a major Broadway and Hollywood musical. One of the reasons why *West Side Story* works so well is that in it Bernstein touches unerringly on something intrinsic to its original: for in scenes like this *Romeo and Juliet is* like a musical. It shares with that genre a tendency to switch suddenly from one dramatic mode to another, to change from naturalistic dialogue into 'lyric' and back again at a moment's notice. Romeo's speech on first seeing Juliet is an aria; his first meeting with her is a duet:

ROMEO

> If I profane with my unworthiest hand
>> This holy shrine, the gentle sin is this.
> My lips, two blushing pilgrims, ready stand
>> To smooth that rough touch with a tender kiss.

JULIET

> Good pilgrim, you do wrong your hand too much,
>> Which mannerly devotion shows in this.
> For saints have hands that pilgrims' hands do touch,
>> And palm to palm is holy palmers' kiss.

ROMEO

Have not saints lips, and holy palmers too?

JULIET

Ay, pilgrim, lips that they must use in prayer.

ROMEO

O, then, dear saint, let lips do what hands do!

  They pray: grant thou, lest faith turn to despair.

JULIET

Saints do not move, though grant for prayers' sake

ROMEO

Then move not while my prayer's effect I take.

(I.5.93–106)

As has frequently been pointed out by critics, scholars and editors, the preceding lines comprise — in dialogue form — a regular Shakespearean sonnet: a fourteen-line poem rhyming ABAB CDCD EFEF GG, divisible into an octave (eight lines) followed by a sestet (six lines), and often embodying some argument, paradox or internal debate which is resolved in the final couplet. And in duet with Juliet, Romeo finds that he is a better poet than he seemed: the sonnet they share is erotic, witty, well structured, complex and coherent. It brings into play a series of logical and rhetorical arguments and paradoxes generated by the juxtaposition of the sacred and profane, and it leads to the satisfactory conclusion of a kiss. Meeting Juliet, Romeo has not left the world of the sonnet sequence: on the contrary, he seems to have found someone who will play the game of love poetry with him, and help him play it better than ever before. When we first saw him he was speaking verse like a minor Elizabethan sonneteer; now he is speaking verse like John Donne.

But Juliet also brings a new perspective to the language of love in the play. The balcony scene (II.2) is a great love scene, and what it focuses on is precisely this relationship between language and love. Both language and love have their private and their communicative dimensions: they deal with inward experience and with relationships between people. It is in this apparent congruence between language and love that Juliet perceives the greatest problem.

Juliet begins the questioning, however, with a more basic exploration into the nature of language:

> O Romeo, Romeo! — Wherefore art thou Romeo?
> Deny thy father and refuse thy name.
>
> . . .
>
> 'Tis but thy name that is my enemy.
> Thou art thyself, though not a Montague.
> What's Montague? It is nor hand nor foot
> Nor arm nor face . . .

(II.2.33–34, 38–41)

What Juliet hints at here has become one of the basic tenets of modern linguistic theory: that word and object have only an arbitrary connection with each other. Linguistics supports Juliet in her assertion that 'That which we call a rose/ By any other word would smell as sweet' — and yet even as Juliet speaks, the inapplicability of the general truth to the particular and pressing instance is evident to the audience. For Juliet's argument does not reach far enough. The logic of linguistics is, here, in conflict with the logic of personal psychology, and Romeo, for all that he might desire it, cannot simply 'doff' his name, any more than Juliet can doff hers. Or rather, it would make no difference if they did. The point is that both Romeo and Juliet are enmeshed, whether they like it or not, in their own, and therefore their families', personal histories. Juliet's target is wrong: it is not the signifier 'Montague', but the signified — a group of people, a network of blood-relationships and a series of events culminating in a bloody feud — which presents the obstacle to their love.

But already Juliet is thinking about the relationship between words and reality. And as she discovers Romeo's presence, and talks to him, it is the language of love itself which obsesses her. And no wonder, for Romeo, still playing the part of the poet, speaks a language which is hard to relate to any observable reality:

> JULIET Art thou not Romeo, and a Montague?
> ROMEO Neither, fair maid, if either thee dislike.

(II.2.60–61)

Just the reply she had desired a few moments earlier! Romeo does indeed offer to doff his name. But Juliet is out of her reverie by this point, and no longer fantasising. More down-to-earth and practical than Romeo, she has realised by now that this is no answer:

> JULIET How camest thou hither, tell me, and wherefore?
>   The orchard walls are high and hard to climb,
>   And the place death, considering who thou art,
>   If any of my kinsmen find thee here.
> ROMEO With love's light wings did I o'erperch these walls.
>   For stony limits cannot hold love out,
>   And what love can do, that dares love attempt.
>   Therefore thy kinsmen are no stop to me.
> JULIET If they do see thee, they will murder thee.
> ROMEO Alack, there lies more peril in thine eye
>   Than twenty of their swords!
>
> (II.2.62–72)

While Romeo weaves his love-poetry metaphors, Juliet's language is severely practical, based on an awareness that in the real world stony limits *can* hold love out, and that the swords of Juliet's kinsmen are infinitely more perilous than are her eyes. It is the difficulty of getting a straight answer out of Romeo, drunk as he is on his own conceits, that leads Juliet into a lecture on the language of love:

> Dost thou love me? I know thou wilt say 'Ay'.
> And I will take thy word. Yet, if thou swearest,
> Thou mayst prove false. At lovers' perjuries,
> They say, Jove laughs. O gentle Romeo,
> If thou dost love, pronounce it faithfully.
>
> (II.2.90–94)

The legendary falseness of lovers' rhetoric is a central issue for Juliet. In love, she implies, truth is a rare commodity, and the language of love is itself a privileged area, outside the normal ethical constraints which prevail: in the language of love, perjury is a trivial crime, and it is not to be expected that words — even the sacred words of oaths — should refer to any material reality. Juliet already knows that Romeo is adept at speaking a language which bears little relation to the real world of walls and swords (and presumably, on one level at least, she is attracted by his extravagant metaphors). But what if that should be all there is to his love? Is there any substance behind the rhetoric? And of course for the audience there is an extra dimension which shows that Juliet's fears are not groundless: Romeo's sonnet-sequence love affair with Rosaline has indeed turned out to be 'lovers' perjuries'.

But Juliet quickly moves from a consideration of the language of Romeo's love to an explanation of her own:

> Or if thou thinkest I am too quickly won,
> I'll frown, and be perverse, and say thee nay,
> So thou wilt woo. But else, not for the world.
> In truth, fair Montague, I am too fond,
> And therefore thou mayst think my 'haviour light.
> But trust me, gentleman, I'll prove more true
> Than those that have more cunning to be strange.
> I should have been more strange, I must confess,
> But that thou overheardest, ere I was ware,
> My true-love passion. Therefore pardon me,
> And not impute this yielding to light love
>
> (II.2.95–105)

The problem is that of sincerity. Juliet does not want to play the part of a disdainful mistress in a courtly-love drama, yet that is one of the roles available to her. Perhaps, too, it is the one that Romeo will best understand. If, on the other hand, she responds in the way that she wants to, by immediately acknowledging to him her feelings, she may be open to the charge of 'light love'. It is part of the rules of the game of courtship in Renaissance Verona that the male is the pursuer, the female the distancer. It is also the logical corollary of Juliet's mistrust of lovers' vows: if passionate affirmation of love often means that there is nothing really there, how should a true lover use language? Should she 'frown and be perverse and say . . . nay'? In order to prove the truth and weightiness of her love, must Juliet avail herself of a rhetoric which denies the existence of that love at all?

She decides not to. Although Juliet has articulated a belief that the language of love is governed by rules almost the opposite of everyday language, she is willing to take the chance that Romeo will understand her. Besides, as she points out, he has overheard her soliloquy, and therefore there is no point in further pretence. The language spoken between lovers may be slippery and full of deceit, but the language which the individual speaks to herself under the impression that nobody is listening is language of another order altogether. That is, language which, by the conventions of the stage at least, represents the truth of the heart. And thus, as she protests her love, Juliet simultaneously anatomises language and analyses the rules governing courtship.

If the balcony scene illustrates anything about the characters of the lovers, it is that the distance between Romeo and Juliet is more than just physical. Juliet's intelligence only goes to show up Romeo's continuing naïvety:

> ROMEO Lady, by yonder blessèd moon I vow,
>   That tips with silver all these fruit-tree tops —
> JULIET O, swear not by the moon, th'inconstant moon,
>   That monthly changes in her circled orb,
>   Lest that thy love prove likewise variable.
> ROMEO What shall I swear by?
> JULIET   Do not swear at all.
>   Or if thou wilt, swear by thy gracious self,
>   Which is the god of my idolatry,
>   And I'll believe thee.

(II.2.107–115)

Romeo still clings to his stock techniques, swearing by the moon as if he had not heard or understood Juliet's previous speech. A sensitive critic, she picks up the connotations of his imagery and rejects it — leaving Romeo a little confused. The moon, after all, is one of the principal props of the sonnet-writer. Deprived of that, he can only ask, 'What shall I swear by?' Juliet, in fact, rejects vows altogether: she has no use for 'specially' true language because she is demanding that all his language be true. She has no use for language which is validated by reference to external touchstones since she demands that Romeo's language be validated by reference to the self.

It is from this point in the play that Romeo's language begins to change. After this scene he is no longer trapped within the rhetorical world of the love sonnet. This comes as a great relief to his friends and relatives:

> MERCUTIO Why, is this not better now than groaning for love?

Now art thou sociable, now art thou Romeo. Now art thou
what thou art, by art as well as by nature. For this drivelling
love is like a great natural that runs lolling up and down to
hide his bauble in a hole.

(II.4.85–90)

Now that he is both loved and in love, Romeo does not have to
put on consciously the role of a lover: the words need no longer
stand for the thing since he has the thing itself. Romeo can now
engage once more in the customary bawdy, witty, competitive
discourse which is the common language of the youth of Verona,
and which finds its apotheosis in Mercutio's punning on his own
death.

Romeo, however, never completely loses his tendency towards flowery rhetoric, but the distance that he has travelled by
the end of the play may best be seen by looking at Act V scene 3.
At the beginning of this scene, two men, both of whom have
courted Juliet and who now believe her to be dead, arrive at her
tomb by night. Each is escorted by a servant with a torch, who is
then sent away. Both then have a short soliloquy. The first to
arrive is the Count Paris:

Sweet flower, with flowers thy bridal bed I strew —
    O woe! thy canopy is dust and stones —
Which with sweet water nightly I will dew;
    Or, wanting that, with tears distilled by moans.
The obsequies that I for thee will keep
Nightly shall be to strew thy grave and weep.

(V.3.12–17)

Paris recites a pretty poem and ritualistically strews flowers on
the grave that is Juliet's 'bridal bed'. The poetry is nothing
special — neither particularly powerful nor particularly inept.
The most that one can say about it is that it is very conventional,
very appropriate, very decorous. It is the sort of poetry which, at
an earlier point in the play, Romeo himself might have spoken
in such a situation.

When Romeo does arrive soon afterwards, both his actions
and the language he uses are anything but decorous: his first
line to his servant is 'Give me that mattock and the wrenching

iron' (V.3.22), and his soliloquy after Balthasar has left has nothing to do with flowers or obsequies:

> Thou detestable maw, thou womb of death,
> Gorged with the dearest morsel of the earth,
> Thus I enforce thy rotten jaws to open,
> And in despite I'll cram thee with more food.

(V.3.45–48)

The violence of this language, the blackness of its wit, the grotesqueness of the image of the grave as a mouth, the dead body as food — all these contrast sharply with Paris's measured tones. It is not that Romeo is not speaking 'poetically': in a sense characters in a Shakespeare play all speak poetically since they all speak the lines of poetry that Shakespeare wrote for them. But the difference between the language of Paris and that of Romeo is the difference between a language which is ready-made for the occasion, and a language which is being invented on the spot, to deal with the pressure of emotion which the situation brings forth. In so many of Shakespeare's plays the question of identity is paramount. Characters forge their own identities, discover themselves, or find old identities destroyed. In *Romeo and Juliet* one of the main ways in which this theme is explored is through the use of language. The love which Romeo and Juliet find is destructive, but it also affirms. Romeo's friends see that he becomes more 'himself' through his love for Juliet. Another way of putting that would be to say that he finds his own voice.

AFTERTHOUGHTS

1

Why should love have developed a special 'language'?

2

Does Mangan's interpretation of Juliet's speech in the light of 'modern linguistic theory' (page 68) raise any interesting issues for you?

3

Do you agree with Mangan's argument that Romeo's language modifies significantly in the course of the play?

4

What *is* one's 'own voice' (page 73)?

John Saunders

John Saunders is Lecturer in English Literature at the West Sussex Institute of Higher Education, and Awarder in English Literature A level for the Oxford and Cambridge Schools Examinations Board.

ESSAY

Time and art

Though 'time' does not in *Romeo and Juliet*, as in *Troilus and Cressida*, become a subject for poetic meditation, its effects are everywhere. They can be seen in old Capulet's avuncular good humour which changes so quickly into choleric bad temper, in the sententious wisdom of the Friar, in Lady Capulet's tired sense of decorum, and in the very aching of the Nurse's head and bones. Contrasts between the vitality of youth and the sluggishness of age abound. Some of these contrasts centre directly or indirectly on attitudes to time: for Juliet, 'in a minute there are many days' (III.5.45), for her Nurse, the most significant moments in Juliet's fourteen years can be condensed into a single rambling, toothless digression. Given the essentially youthful quality of Romeo and Juliet's love, it can be argued that the forces which conspire to destroy it do in fact preserve their love by saving it from the tyranny of time. And what of those forces? Though the play's rhetoric is insistent that Romeo and Juliet are 'star-crossed lovers', both the language of foreboding and the many accompanying accidents in timing which lead to their eventual deaths can be seen to derive not from a genuinely malignant sense of fate but from the manipulative art of the dramatist. Through Shakespeare's art, Romeo and Juliet have been granted a form of immortality, living on in legend as exemplars of young love. In the essay which follows, I want to concentrate my analysis on the scene in which the lovers meet at the Capulet ball. This is the scene in which the destructive power of time and the timelessness of art are given their most concrete poetic and dramatic expression.

Present, past and future meet in the ballroom scene. Well before it commences, it has become a focal point of interest for both major and minor characters, all of whom look to the occasion with very different motivations. For the Capulet family the ball may prove instrumental in prolonging the dynasty by obtaining a husband for Juliet. Juliet's father describes the ball to Paris as an 'old accustomed feast' (I.2.20), implying that it is but one of the series of established family rituals. But this feast is to be of especial significance, since it will mark Juliet's entry into adult society. She will take her place for the first time among the other 'admirèd beauties of Verona' (I.2.83), a public acknowledgement of her marital status. Paris, and any other suitors who have decided that Capulet's wealth and social standing make her a desirable match, will at last be able to see her. The notion that the occasion is to be a kind of spring ritual, a rite of passage through which Juliet will move from childhood to maturity, is further enforced by Capulet's image of 'fresh female buds', on display for the pleasure of 'lusty young men' (I.2.29,26). There is, however, a suggestion that even at this moment he is reluctant to accept that Juliet is fully ready for marriage. 'Let two more summers wither in their pride/ Ere we may think her ripe to be a bride' (I.2.10–11), he tells Paris. When in the next scene Lady Capulet broaches the subject of marriage with Juliet, she seems unaware of her husband's misgivings. In fact she sees her own example as having established the desirability of early marriage: 'By my count,/ I was your mother much upon these years/ That you are now a maid' (I.3.72–74). For the audience this revelation may ironically echo Capulet's earlier wry comment that young women who marry too young are 'too soon marred' (I.2.13). Moreover, in the artificiality and inappropriateness of the laboured conceit with which Lady Capulet attempts to interest Juliet in Paris — comparing him to 'a precious book', that 'only lacks a cover' (I.3.88–89) — she gives the impression that through marrying too young she has had little experience of the potential passion of youth. The Juliet whom the audience glimpse in this scene is quite different from the Juliet who is about to blossom. She is completely malleable, a dutiful daughter, programmed into looking on marriage as an undreamed of 'honour' (I.3.67) and determined to do her best to please her mother:

> I'll look to like, if looking liking move.
> But no more deep will I endart mine eye
> Than your consent gives strength to make it fly.

> (I.3.98–100)

The final member of the Capulet household, the Nurse, sees Juliet's blossoming only in terms of crude sexuality. She looks on the ball as a step towards Juliet's loss of virginity: 'Go, girl, seek happy nights to happy days' (I.3.106).

The maskers, too, have differing expectations from the ball. Benvolio decides to risk attending so that he can cure Romeo of his infatuation with Rosaline by showing him that in comparison with other beauties his 'swan' will seem 'a crow' (I.2.86). Mercutio would seem to see the ball as providing an opportunity for a youthful escapade, though he too is determined to cure Romeo, there being a kind of medicine in his mockery. Finally, there is Romeo's much more complex set of responses. Though he agrees to accompany Benvolio so that he can 'rejoice' in Rosaline's 'splendour' (I.2.100), his 'soul of lead' (I.4.15) is not in keeping with the frivolity of Mercutio and the other maskers. When the company are urged to hurry — 'Supper is done, and we shall come too late' (I.4.105) — Romeo's ponderous reply ensures that the events of the ball will be placed firmly within the poetic framework of fate, which is foregrounded throughout the play:

> I fear, too early. For my mind misgives
> Some consequence, yet hanging in the stars,
> Shall bitterly begin his fearful date
> With this night's revels and expire the term
> Of a despisèd life, closed in my breast,
> By some vile forfeit of untimely death.

> (I.4.106–111)

The ballroom scene itself begins with a short section of dialogue between a group of Capulet's servants. The flexibility of the conventions of the Elizabethan stage would have required these 'Servingmen' to make minor alterations to props in order to translate the setting from a street to a banqueting hall. However, this is not their only function. Their short sequence of dialogue (I.5.1–16) provides a vivid glimpse of life 'below stairs', with its petty rivalries ('Where's Potpan, that he helps not to take away'), with its humour ('When good manners shall lie all in one or two men's hands, and they unwashed too') and with its own potential love intrigues ('as thou lovest me, let the porter let in Susan Grindstone and Nell'). In so doing, this dialogue serves as a bridge from melancholy to festivity, distancing Romeo's sense of foreboding from the mood of the ball. Less obviously, but more importantly, the briskness of the Servingmen's chatter and their impression of bustle ('Away with the joint-stools; remove the court-cupboard; look to the plate' . . . 'You are looked for and called for, asked for and sought for, in the Great Chamber' . . . 'We cannot be here and there too. Cheerly, boys! Be brisk a while, and the longer liver take all') serve as a foil to the more leisured, stately entrance of Capulet and his guests as they prepare to welcome the maskers. The suggestion of urgency in this short episode is one of a number of features which contribute to the masterly manipulation of time which characterises the scene as it progresses.

When Capulet and his principal guests enter, the evening is still relatively young. The host, having dined well, is in an expansive mood. First he greets the 'ladies' with a good-humoured joke:

> Welcome, gentlemen! Ladies that have their toes
> Unplagued with corns will walk a bout with you.

> (I.5.17–18)

It is the kind of joke with which many a middle-aged father might, unintentionally, make his young daughter shudder. In case anyone has missed the humour, he proceeds to provide his own laborious explanation:

> Ah, my mistresses, which of you all
> Will now deny to dance? She that makes dainty,
> She, I'll swear, hath corns.

> (I.5.19–21)

Two mentions of 'corns' in five lines tells us more — of course —

of Capulet than of the anonymous ladies he is addressing. Old Capulet knows he is well past his 'dancing days' (I.5.32), but he is a master in his own house whose jokes must be respected. This may be some slight consolation for a lost youth and for a life in which all 'hopes', other than Juliet, have been 'swallowed' (I.2.14). He turns to welcome the 'gentlemen', and begins to indulge in nostalgia, remembering his own escapades as a masker:

> Welcome, gentlemen! I have seen the day
> That I have worn a visor and could tell
> A whispering tale in a fair lady's ear,
> Such as would please.
>
> (I.5.22–25)

These lines do more than just provide an image from Capulet's distant past. They look forward to the central moment of the scene, where Romeo, wearing his 'visor', will win Juliet's heart through whispered words of love. For Capulet, the memory exists as a painful reminder of the loss of his own youth: "Tis gone, 'tis gone, 'tis gone!' (I.5.25). For the audience, the image may serve as a reminder that, without 'fate's' intervention, Romeo might one day be old too and, with a similar combination of nostalgia and regret, look back on the evening when he met Juliet.

Having welcomed ladies and gentlemen, Capulet calls for music, and dancing begins. In the Elizabethan theatre the dancing and music would have been formal, a stately expression of harmony and social order. On any stage, music and dancing unaccompanied by dialogue represent a break with the conventions of naturalistic time. When Capulet continues to speak, his orders to his servants indicate that time has passed — 'More light . . . quench the fire, the room is grown too hot' (I.5.28–29). Then, as he talks more intimately with an elderly cousin, the topic of time and the speed of its passing dominates their conversation. In attempting to remember when they last danced, the two old men struggle with the arithmetic of time, measuring their lives in terms of family weddings and festivals. When the old cousin tells him the age of Lucentio's son, we realise that Capulet's earlier bright image of his own masking has lasted 'thirty years'. And Capulet's remonstration — 'His son was but a ward two years ago' (I.5.41) — is, surely, not intended as a contradiction but as an exclamation on the relativity of time: in what seems like a mere two years, many years have passed.

The old men's duet on time is broken abruptly as the focus shifts to Romeo, who has just seen Juliet and fallen in love with her in an instant. For a moment time seems to stand still, the naturalistic dialogue of the elderly Capulets giving way to Romeo's rhyming verse as he delivers a panegyric on Juliet's beauty:

> O, she doth teach the torches to burn bright!
> It seems she hangs upon the cheek of night
> As a rich jewel in an Ethiop's ear —
> Beauty too rich for use, for earth too dear!
>
> (I.5.44–47)

For some readers, these lines might seem too opulent, too close to cliché, too like Romeo's earlier love-sick rhyming. Perhaps they are intended to mark the beginning of Romeo's metamorphosis. But, unlike the abstract, rather shallow praising of Rosaline's beauty, the language here has a concrete dramatic focus. It accompanies Romeo's gazing on Juliet and she, not the words, should be central. Moreover, this first description of Juliet has a wider poetic and thematic significance. In the strangely ornate image of Juliet hanging 'upon the cheek of night/ As a rich jewel in an Ethiop's ear', there is the first of a series of images linking her beauty to the permanent loveliness of the heavens. But the imagery also enforces the sense of Juliet's transience (she burns, like the torches) and her beauty's vulnerability ('Beauty too rich for use, for earth too dear').

The potential fragility of Romeo's new-found love is starkly focused by what immediately follows, the 'ancient grudge' of the two families threatening their future as the feud finds fresh expression in the anger of Tybalt, who has recognised Romeo's voice. Tybalt's passionate hatred parallels Romeo's passionate love. Both are expressed in rhyming verse. While the dancing continues and Romeo moves to position himself where he will be able to engage with Juliet, Tybalt spits out his enmity to his uncle:

> A villain, that is hither come in spite

To scorn at our solemnity this night.

(I.5.62–63)

Though Capulet's initial response is moderate — 'Content thee, gentle coz, let him alone' (I.5.65) — and there is a momentary sense that the festive spirit might lead to a new harmony between the families, Capulet, too, breaks into a fit of temper when his nephew crosses him. And though the conflict between the young man and his uncle leads to the departure of Tybalt, providing a moment of respite for Romeo and Juliet, we have seen in their anger what will emerge as a dual threat to the lovers. The quickness with which Capulet, when crossed, moves from affability to violent temper will later play its part in the tragedy when he insists that Juliet must obey him and marry Paris. Tybalt's threat is more obviously dramatic and the encounter about to take place between Romeo and Juliet is framed by the venom of his final couplet:

> I will withdraw. But this intrusion shall,
> Now seeming sweet, convert to bitterest gall.

(I.5.91–92)

The hint given earlier that Romeo sees himself as a pilgrim and Juliet as a saint — 'And, touching hers, make blessèd my rude hand' (I.5.51) — provides the central conceit for the love duet which follows. Though the form and language of the exchange are elaborately artificial, the tone of the lovers' meeting marks the birth of a new Romeo and a new Juliet. Gone is the melancholy, leaden-souled parody of a young lover; gone, too, are all traces of the compliant, passive daughter. Romeo emerges as a daring, witty and accomplished courtier. Juliet matches his wit, teasing him with her answers without restraining him. No kiss in literature has been more cleverly contrived. The love game (I.5.93–107) takes the form of a perfect Shakespearean sonnet. In the first quatrain, Romeo takes Juliet's hand, suggests that the touching of this 'holy shrine' is a sin, and offers his lips as 'blushing pilgrims' who can kiss the hand and so absolve the sin. In Juliet's answering quatrain, she says that there is no need for kissing since both pilgrims and saints have hands and for pilgrims (palmers) who visit holy shrines, the touching of the saint's hand is a form of kissing: 'And palm to palm is holy palmers' kiss'. So ends the octave of the sonnet. In the third quatrain, Romeo's suggestion that saints and palmers have lips — which might be used in kissing — is parried by Juliet's answer that in religious quests lips are for praying, not kissing. The quatrain ends with Romeo using his lips to pray that Juliet grant his request (for a kiss) to prevent his faith from turning to 'despair' — a state of sin. In the final couplet, Juliet invites Romeo to kiss her by suggesting that though she — as the statue of a saint — can grant his prayer, she is unable to 'move' to him. The sonnet ends as Romeo moves to her (kissing her) and taking his 'prayer's effect'.

The first kiss prayed for, granted and taken, the lovers commence on a second sonnet but they are interrupted by the croaking of the Nurse who tells Juliet that her mother wishes to speak to her. The Nurse has watched their meeting — 'I nursed her daughter that you talked withal' (I.5.115) — and, not knowing Romeo's identity, sees him as a potential suitor. 'I tell you, he that can lay hold of her/ Shall have the chinks' (I.5.116–117) she tells him, the crudeness of her language revealing that in her eyes young men need more than love to tempt them into marriage. With the Nurse's intrusion, the magical moment is destroyed and, as Romeo and Juliet ponder separately on the portentous significance of their love, the party comes to an end and the guests disperse. In some ten or fifteen minutes of dramatic time a whole evening has passed.

Why does Shakespeare contrive that the lovers' first meeting takes the form of a dramatised sonnet? When writing *Romeo and Juliet*, Shakespeare was much preoccupied with the sonnet form. Sonnets, part sonnets and partial sonnets occur throughout the text of the play. Most noticeably, the first Act begins and ends with Choruses in sonnet form. In Shakespeare's own *Sonnet* sequence, many of whose poems were written shortly before and after the writing of *Romeo and Juliet*, there are two recurring themes which may help to answer the question. The first is a concern with the destructive power of time, which is pictured variously in the sonnets as a 'bloody tyrant', as a ravening animal and — more conventionally — as a mower. A counter-theme is the recurring idea that poetry — in particular, the sonnet itself — has the potential to transcend time. Sonnet 18, for example, ends with the assertion that the subject of the poem's praise will be granted a form of immortality by the poem:

> So long as men can breathe or eyes can see,
> So long lives this, and this gives life to thee.

And the next sonnet in the sequence links love, time and poetry in its final couplet:

> Yet do thy worst, old Time: despite thy wrong
> My love shall in my verse ever live young.

I think that these somewhat abstract ideas about Art's relationship to Time find their finest concrete expression in the scene I have discussed where — though never crudely stated — the image of the lovers' meeting has an imaginative permanence which is highlighted by the various ways in which time's passing is dramatised throughout the scene. What is more, the play ends in a partial sonnet which both mirrors the first meeting of the lovers and reinforces the idea that art has the power to transcend time. First Capulet asks Montague to give him his hand. Then, presumably still holding hands, Montague, speaking in rhyming verse, resolves to commission the raising of a 'pure gold' statue of Juliet to commemorate her truth and faithfulness. Capulet, also speaking in rhyme, promises to join in the enterprise: 'As rich shall Romeo's by his lady lie,/ Poor sacrifices of our enmity!' (V.3.303–304). Then, in what is in fact the concluding sestet of a sonnet, the Prince announces the beginning of 'A glooming peace' (V.3.305), suggesting in the play's final rhyming couplet that the lovers will become the subject of legend:

> For never was a story of more woe
> Than this of Juliet and her Romeo.
>
> (V.3.309–310)

And Shakespeare's play is, of course, only one of many retellings of the 'story'.

AFTERTHOUGHTS

1

What relationship between art and time is suggested in the first paragraph of this essay?

2

Why does Saunders claim that 'Present, past and future meet in the ballroom scene' (page 76)?

3

Do you agree that 'the tone of the lovers' meeting marks the birth of a new Romeo and a new Juliet' (page 81)?

4

Explain the significance to Saunders's argument of his analysis of the play's ending (page 83).

Susie Campbell

Susie Campbell is Head of English at the North Westminster School. She is the author of several critical studies.

ESSAY

Blind Cupid and death

The deaths of the young lovers at the end of *Romeo and Juliet* are necessary not only to purge Verona of the dark forces of violence and hatred that have been let loose on its streets, but also to satisfy the audience. For all our sympathy with the tragic pair of young lovers, if we are denied their deaths at the end, we feel cheated. The sentimental Victorian productions of the play in which the lovers live on to enjoy a happy ending seem, to the modern audience, farcical. This is because the deaths of Romeo and Juliet are indissolubly linked to their love for each other. However, this is not to suggest that Romeo and Juliet actively seek death as the proper fulfilment of their love. M M Mahood, in *Shakespeare's Wordplay* (London, 1957), effectively answers those critics who have argued that the love of Romeo and Juliet is the tragic passion that seeks its own destruction. She reminds us that the tragedy of the play springs largely from the thwarting of the young lovers' attempts to escape death and live on together. Their love is not, she argues, by its nature tragic, even if it has tragic consequences.

Of course, one obvious reason for the audience's sense that the love and deaths of the lovers are somehow linked could be their conventional poetic pairing. Love and Death were particularly popular as a pair of twin motifs in Elizabethan sonnets and love poems. They occur, for example, throughout Sir Philip

Sidney's sonnet sequence *Astrophel and Stella*. Sonnet XX begins: 'Fly, fly, my friends — I have my death wound — fly!' Less well known but equally representative, Thomas Lodge uses the image of love waging war upon his heart:

> For pity, pretty eyes, surcease
> To give me war, and grant me peace!

The second verse extends the motif:

> Will you, alas, command me die?
> Then die I yours, and death my cross;
> But unto you pertains the loss.

Throughout *Romeo and Juliet*, Shakespeare uses the twin conventions of love and death. The sexual pun on 'dying' for love allows Mercutio free rein for much of his bawdy jesting. At the very beginning of the play, Romeo himself, talking of Rosaline, says to Benvolio:

> She hath forsworn to love; and in that vow
> Do I live dead that live to tell it now.

> (I.1.223–224)

However, the conventions that Romeo draws on here are shown up to be formulaic and trite when he meets Juliet. One of the ironies of the play is the way that the hyperbolic talk of love as a 'wound' at the beginning of the play has turned into a tragic reality by the end. The fact that Shakespeare draws on what were, by his time, rather overworked and outworn conventions only to contrast them with the more powerful and deeply felt nature of Romeo's later feelings for Juliet suggests that they are not the real source of the audience's sense of the inevitability of the play's tragic ending.

But, alongside these outworn poetic conventions, is another, much older vein of linked imagery. It is through this other, more potent tradition, I suggest, that Shakespeare forges a network of macabre links between the dark destiny opposing the lovers' happiness and their love itself. It is this network, whose connections are rarely made explicit or obvious, that suggests that Romeo and Juliet's love and deaths are inextricably linked.

The key to the presence of this older tradition is the idea of blindness. The play is full of references to, and images of, blindness or blindfolded vision. In particular, the relationship between the two young lovers is figured in terms of a loss of sight. Even before they meet, Benvolio urges Romeo to:

> Take thou some new infection to thy eye,
> And the rank poison of the old will die.

(I.2.49–50)

Juliet falls in love with Romeo 'blind'. She has already lost her heart to the stranger before she finds out who he is: 'Too early seen unknown, and known too late' (I.5.139). The cover of darkness under which most of Romeo and Juliet's meetings take place is linked, by Benvolio, to blindness. Jesting with Mercutio, he laughs, 'Blind is his love, and best befits the dark' (II.1.32). Romeo comes to Juliet, in the balcony scene, 'bescreened in night' (II.2.52), escapes his enemies by wearing 'night's cloak to hide me from their eyes' (II.2.75), and identifies himself with the figure of Blind Cupid: 'He lent me counsel, and I lent him eyes' (II.2.81). More seriously, Juliet invokes all the powers of Night to confer its own particular blindness on the world so that the lovers can enjoy their love in secrecy. More potently than Benvolio, Juliet recognises and validates the link between blind love and the night:

>   . . . if love be blind,
> It best agrees with night.

(III.2.9–10)

And she welcomes, 'Come, civil night' (III.2.10). But it is only at the end of the play that the sinister significance of all these references to blindness and darkness becomes clear, as the presence of the other sightless companion of Blind Cupid and Night is revealed. This companion is Death, whose 'eyeless skulls' (V.3.126) litter the Capulet tomb where the last tragic scenes are played out.

The tradition that Shakespeare draws on here is very old. It has its roots in a medieval iconography in which Cupid was linked with Night, Death and Fortune. The familiar, playful figure of Cupid as a mischievous boy was a later, Renaissance development in which the idea of his blindness had ceased to mean much more than the unpredictability of love's choices. The blindness of the medieval Cupid had a much more serious meaning. In his *Medieval Iconography* (New York, 1939), Panofsky shows how, to the medieval mind, Cupid's blindness represented the dangerous random forces and the moral darkness of uncontrollable passions. It was through this moral 'blindness' that he was linked with the other sinister forces that govern men's lives, Death, Night and Fortune — the blind puppet-masters of humankind.

In *Romeo and Juliet*, I suggest, Shakespeare reaches back past the contemporary conventions linking love and death to draw on the power of this older, grimmer iconography. Whilst the Renaissance had reworked and changed many of these old traditions, they had not been forgotten. In Act I of *A Midsummer Night's Dream*, written almost contemporaneously with *Romeo and Juliet* and making comic mileage out of love's blindness, Helena shows an understanding of some of the old moral significance of the figure of Blind Cupid:

> Love looks not with the eyes, but with the mind,
> And therefore is winged Cupid painted blind.
> Nor hath love's mind of any judgement taste;
> Wings and no eyes figure unheedy haste.

(I.1.234–237)

Her last words are reminiscent of Friar Laurence's warnings in *Romeo and Juliet*. The Friar is one of the characters in the play who shows himself to be acquainted with the ancient lore and customs, and evokes an older, sterner tradition about the dangers of blind passion.

In the world of *Romeo and Juliet*, it is only the older folk who have any real belief in the old customs. To the younger generation, they are simply old-fashioned ideas. Benvolio reminds his companions, on their way to Capulet's ball, that times have changed. There is now no place for old customs and traditions:

> The date is out of such prolixity.
> We'll have no Cupid hoodwinked with a scarf,
> Bearing a Tartar's painted bow of lath,
> Scaring the ladies like a crowkeeper

(I.4.3–6)

Mercutio makes a joke out of the figure of Blind Cupid and his association with Death:

> Alas, poor Romeo, he is already dead! — stabbed with a white wench's black eye, run through the ear with a love song; the very pin of his heart cleft with the blind bow-boy's butt-shaft. And is he a man to encounter Tybalt?
>
> (II.4.13–17)

However, Mercutio's attitude to the old traditions is ambiguous. His attempt to debunk other old superstitious beliefs reveals his reluctant fascination with their power. As he attempts to empty out the popular tales about Queen Mab, he becomes caught up in their imaginative potency, and Romeo has to interrupt him to break the spell:

> MERCUTIO This is the hag, when maids lie on their backs,
> That presses them and learns them first to bear,
> Making them women of good carriage.
> This is she —
> ROMEO Peace, peace, Mercutio, peace.
> Thou talk'st of nothing.
>
> (I.4.92–96)

Ironically, Mercutio doesn't know what he knows. Playfully invoking Blind Cupid, he interferes with the tangled dark forces that link the fates of Romeo, Juliet and Tybalt, and meets his own death.

There is similar dramatic irony as both Romeo and Juliet call on the old powers of Night, Death and Fate, like children unknowingly invoking old, terrible powers. Brian Gibbons, in his Introduction to the Arden edition of the play, emphasises the child-like nature of Juliet's speech to Night in Act III:

> Juliet speaks directly from her young heart, revealing her poignant prematurity when she gives mythological figures of such mystery and authority as Cupid and Night these practical, domestic, humble jobs: drawing curtains, teaching a child to play a game, hooding a falcon, cutting stars out of silver paper.
>
> (page 59)

It is only at the end of the play that Romeo and Juliet finally confront the grim powers they have recklessly and naïvely invoked. Juliet, about to take the sleeping potion, fears that she will wake up prematurely and will be driven mad by the 'horrible conceit of death and night,/ Together with the terror of the place' (IV.3.37–38), whilst Romeo, broaching the Capulets' tomb, comes face to face with the horror of mortality:

> Thou detestable maw, thou womb of death,
> Gorged with the dearest morsel of the earth,
> Thus I enforce thy rotten jaws to open,
> And in despite I'll cram thee with more food.

> (V.3.45–48)

Romeo, who laid down the bold challenge, 'Then love-devouring death do what he dare' (II.6.7), failed to recognise that Death has been, all along, one of his own masked companions.

And so Shakespeare prepares the audience for the final deaths of the young lovers by the macabre association with which their love has been surrounded from the start. But does this subtle yet potent network of associations have any deeper significance within the play?

One of the most striking aspects of the play is the way that the two young lovers become increasingly isolated. They leave behind the tight circles of family and friends in order to be with each other and enjoy their own private world, swearing to disavow their own family names. Even before he meets Juliet, Romeo is something of an individualist. He steals off on his own to dream of Rosaline. Throughout the play, we see the lovers separating themselves from their companions. Romeo hides himself from his friends after the ball; Juliet sends away her Nurse; Romeo dismisses Balthasar at the tomb; Juliet bids Friar Laurence: 'Go, get thee hence' (V.3.160). When they are together, the lovers create an intimate world from which they attempt to shut out external reality and the forces that threaten them.

But the community from which Romeo and Juliet attempt to separate themselves will not give up its young heirs lightly. Romeo's companions attempt to hold him within the group. For all his own eccentricity, Mercutio is keen to hold on to the Romeo he knows and recognises. 'Now art thou sociable. Now art thou Romeo' (II.4.87), he exults when Romeo once again takes part in the bawdy jesting that is an important part of the adolescent peer-bond of this group of young men. Old Montague feels that his son's desire for solitude is unnatural and ominous. 'Black and portentous must this humour prove' (I.1.141), he worries at the beginning of the play. By evoking an old super-stitious tradition of imagery, I suggest, Shakespeare gives imaginative realisation to these fears. To stand alone was an unlucky and dangerous thing. All the unknown forces of the Elizabethan universe that might be offended by a human arrogantly acting as an individual are imaged in the blind powers that oppose Romeo and Juliet's happiness. Nor is this mere superstition on Shakespeare's part. It is one way of giving poetic expression to all the powerful community forces that knit together a society and control the individuals within it. Because, of course, ultimately it is these social forces — not the abstract forces of Death and Fortune — that bring about the tragic ending.

Romeo and Juliet have to separate themselves from the claims of family and community in order to resist the whole bitter history of feuding and hatred. But, in so doing, they set themselves against not only the powerful forces that define that various different social groups of Verona but also the whole weight of culture and tradition of the community itself. Shakespeare gives imaginative expression to these forces by evoking all the old demons of the night against which a com-munity supposedly protected its individual members.

Significantly, as Romeo and Juliet step outside their com-munity, they find themselves in opposition, particularly, to the old ways and traditions. Their very first meeting is set against the old men's reminiscences of old Capulet and Cousin Capulet. Old Capulet says:

> I have seen the day
> That I have worn a visor and could tell
> A whispering tale in a fair lady's ear,
> Such as would please. 'Tis gone, 'tis gone, 'tis gone!

> (I.5.22–25)

Both Romeo and Juliet are irritated by the slowness and caution of old age. Romeo answers Friar Laurence's advice to be more moderate with the retort: 'Thou canst not speak of that thou dost not feel' (III.3.65), and Juliet, impatient with the slowness of the Nurse, complains:

> ... old folks, many feign as they were dead —
> Unwieldy, slow, heavy and pale as lead.
>
> (II.5.16–17)

But it is these very old folk who carry the memory and traditions of communal knowledge. It is to the Nurse that Lady Capulet applies for information about the family. By opposing them, Romeo and Juliet are setting themselves against the shared beliefs and values of the community as well as their own family history and culture. Shakespeare represents this dramatically in Juliet nerving herself to take the sleeping potion. It is not just death that appals her: it is the whole terror of her ancestors and family inheritance. She describes the vault as:

> ... an ancient receptacle
> Where for this many hundred years the bones
> Of all my buried ancestors are packed
>
> (IV.3.39–41)

In the end, the combined power of these forces is too much for the lovers and they are overwhelmed by them. Shakespeare is not optimistic about the fate of those who attempt to take on such adversaries. It is the claims of family name and group loyalty that finally reassert themselves and lead to Romeo killing Tybalt, the act that precipitates the final tragedy. But, ironically, while the community opposes those who attempt to step outside it, it is through the sacrifice of those very individuals that communal health is restored. Unwittingly, Romeo and Juliet unleash the deep, mysterious forces that hold together the fabric of their community. But through their own identification with and defiance of these forces, they purge them of their negative, destructive energies and enable ancient rifts to be healed.

At the end of the play, all is open and visible. The tomb is laid open and 'these ambiguities' (V.3.217) are cleared. The dark powers of the night have retreated and the community is restored to 'glooming peace' (V.3.305). Through their own fierce passion, Romeo and Juliet have stirred up the deep, enigmatic energies that lie at the roots of community and, by their deaths, have transformed them into a new cohesive force.

1

Explain the significance of the description of the medieval Cupid (pages 87–88) to the argument of this essay.

2

Does *Romeo and Juliet* as a whole challenge or sustain 'ancient lore and customs' (page 88)?

3

Does all tragedy involve isolation (see page 90)?

4

What arguments about the power and importance of community are put forward in this essay? How far do you agree?

Angus Alton

Angus Alton works as a researcher for the University of Oxford Delegacy of Local Examinations. He is also an experienced examiner in English Literature at GCSE and A level.

ESSAY

Fate, responsibility and blame

Romeo and Juliet has always been one of the easiest of Shakespeare's plays to study for examination. This is partly because the basic plot is so straightforward and appealing, which makes the fact of study much less of a chore. But it is also partly a result of the fact that it is almost inconceivable to examine pupils' understanding of the play without giving them the opportunity to show how familiar they are with the notion that Romeo and Juliet's story is one that shows how human intentions can be thwarted by a seemingly malignant fate.

It is an easy enough line to take with the play. Few people can read or, especially, watch it without being powerfully struck by a feeling of 'if only': a sense that, almost to the very end, events could easily turn out quite differently. In the last analysis, it is not in fact a view that I find very helpful, and the purpose of this essay is to show a different way of looking at how things happen in the play. However, it is important, first, to acknowledge that there are powerful arguments in favour of the view that the tragedy really is the story of 'star-crossed lovers' (Prologue, line 6).

There are, essentially, three main aspects of the interpretation. The first of these derives from the nature of the plot itself.

There is no disputing that the play contains many coincidences and pieces of unfortunate timing. From the moment when Capulet's illiterate servant chooses Romeo and his friends to help him read the names on his master's guest list in Act I scene 2 to the 'accident' (V.3.251) which detained Friar John and prevented him delivering the letter which would have given Romeo the background to Juliet's 'death', there is a steady sequence of developments in which ill fortune must be seen as the principal if not the only factor. Indeed, much of the play's power over an audience comes from the impulse it creates, as in melodrama or pantomime, to wish to participate, to call out, as it were, 'look out behind you!'; in *Romeo and Juliet*, however, we are beset by a sense that there is nothing very specific to look out for, no villain creeping up. Thus, Friar John's delay would be no serious problem were it not that Capulet has impulsively brought forward the date for his daughter's marriage to Paris. Conversely, even a slight delay — perhaps a longer fight with Paris — would have been enough for Friar Laurence to arrive at the Capulet tomb in time to prevent Romeo's swallowing the 'soon-speeding gear' (V.1.60) he has obtained from the Apothecary. It must also be remembered that Mercutio's death, which can be taken as the point of no return in the play — for the death prevents the possibility of a happy ending — is to an extent an unlucky accident.

In addition to the chapter of misfortunes which constitutes an important element in the plot, the language of the play regularly encourages the audience to see events as dominated by fate. Indeed, I hope it is not mischievous to suggest that the availability of quotable lines which suggest this is partly responsible for the frequency with which the topic appears on examination papers. From the reference to 'star-crossed lovers' already quoted from the first Chorus, examples abound. Romeo picks up the reference to the stars in his final speech:

> O here
> Will I set up my everlasting rest
> And shake the yoke of inauspicious stars
> From this world-wearied flesh

> (V.3.109–112)

while the simple piety of Friar Laurence and of Romeo's line:

> But He that hath the steerage of my course
> Direct my sail!
>
> (I.4.112–113)

seem cruelly ironic in the light of what happens.

At the same time, the play is filled with ominous speeches. These take several different forms. In the first place, there is the kind of comment in which the speaker consciously suggests that all is not well. Pre-eminent among these is the sequence in Act I scene 4 where Romeo and Mercutio discuss dreams. We never actually learn the content of the dream that Romeo claims to have had: the ridicule of Mercutio's Queen Mab speech prevents that. But what Romeo then says suggests that his dream some-how foretold his fate:

> For my mind misgives
> Some consequence, yet hanging in the stars,
> Shall bitterly begin his fearful date
> With this night's revels and expire the term
> Of a despisèd life, closed in my breast,
> By some vile forfeit of untimely death.
>
> (I.4.106–111)

As well as these specific omens, the play also contains rather more generalised comments, which, nevertheless, serve to suggest that all will not turn out for the best. Twice, Friar Laurence gives voice to warnings which have such an effect. First, he responds to Romeo's impatient haste by warning him, 'They stumble that run fast' (II.3.90), and later he gives voice to a similar sentiment in the face of Romeo's overpowering passion for Juliet:

> These violent delights have violent ends
> And in their triumph die, like fire and powder,
> Which as they kiss consume.
>
> (II.6.9–11)

It must also be noted that the tendency of the play to make Friar Laurence the repository of much of its wisdom, sympathy and understanding gives such warnings an even greater ominous aspect.

The other main way in which the language serves to suggest

that matters are outside human control comes from the familiar Shakespearean trick of dramatic irony. The regularity with which Romeo and Juliet's love is seen in terms of death and pain insistently keeps the tragic outcome of the play before our eyes. This doesn't just work at the level of lines which have obvious implications, as when Romeo tells Juliet 'there lies more peril in thine eye/ Than twenty of their swords' (II.2.91–92). It also features more subtly when Juliet is being consciously ironic about Tybalt's death and the punishment of his killer:

> Madam, if you could find out but a man
> To bear a poison, I would temper it —
> That Romeo should, upon receipt thereof,
> Soon sleep in quiet.

(III.5.96–99)

The language of the play, then, does much to encourage the idea that what happens in *Romeo and Juliet* is fated. But, perhaps the most powerful aspect of the play in terms of this view lies in the characters. Quite simply, *Romeo and Juliet* is a tragedy without a villain, and this makes it much harder to see the play in the familiar terms of the antagonistic qualities in human nature. In *Othello* and in *Hamlet*, we have Iago and Claudius to embody something very close to pure evil; in *Macbeth*, we see that evil itself in the weird sisters, and *King Lear* is abundantly supplied with thoroughly nasty characters. But in this play, almost everybody acts from essentially good motives.

This is not to suggest that the characters are faultless. Tybalt's absurd strutting and quarrelsomeness make him a distinctly unattractive figure, and Mercutio, although much more likeable, is, as Benvolio suggest in Act III scene 1, far too apt to quarrel. Capulet, too, headstrong and quick-tempered, is hardly an ideal figure, and even the servants are shown to be aggressive, albeit in a rather ludicrous way. But none of these characters exhibit qualities that make one think in terms of evil rather than of faults. Indeed, the key point is that the *intentions* in every case are undeniably for the best. Tybalt, although almost certainly angry at having been told off by Capulet, is principally seeking to avenge what he sees as the slight on the family honour caused by Romeo's presence at the feast. Mercutio is reacting to very real insults to the Montagues and what he sees as Romeo's inexplicable refusal to take up the challenge. And Capulet not only shows considerable generosity when Romeo is identified within his house, but he certainly believes he is acting in his daughter's best interests both in his choice of husband and in his desire to conclude the marriage quickly. Curiously, perhaps the most telling example of the absence of any sense of evil — whether supernatural or human — can be found in one of the most minor characters. The Apothecary from whom Romeo buys his poison seems at first to provide an ideal opportunity at least to glance at malice and corruption; instead, we glimpse a social problem: a man driven to act against his conscience by neediness:

> My poverty but not my will consents.
>
> (V.1.75)

The usual assumption made as a result of these arguments is that, since no one can be shown to be the focus of evil within the play, since the characters can, at worst, be accused of venial faults, then the tragic outcome must have been caused by misfortune. In short, the odds were stacked against the unlucky couple. It is an assumption that I believe needs careful examination before it is allowed to stand: perhaps, it cannot be allowed to stand at all.

There are several aspects of the play which such a view tends to ignore, and, in the last analysis, these aspects are surely crucial ones. Principally, it simply is not true that the main events of the play are a result of bad luck. I have already mentioned that Mercutio's death can be seen as the main impulse of the tragic action of the play, and that it is to some extent an accident. But, to what extent? It is probably the case that the inflated sense of pride that both Tybalt and Mercutio exhibit seems even more absurd to a modern audience than it did to Shakespeare's contemporaries, but there can be little doubt that it *was* absurd then too. Much of the early part of the play illustrates the various posturings of adolescents. Whether it be Romeo's mock-love of Rosaline, Mercutio's mockery of the Nurse, the overblown witticisms that flow between Mercutio and Romeo, we are very much conscious that these are people who are becoming aware of their nature as autonomous beings, but who have not yet quite worked out how to give this awareness effective articulation. Surely, despite its fatal consequences, the trading of insults that leads up to the fight is to be seen in the same light. It is certainly hard to see the fight as *necessary*, and thus the outcome equally lacks any sense of inevitability.

Even if it didn't, how far is Romeo's reaction to be seen as desirable? It is important here to distinguish between our understanding and, even, sympathy for Romeo in his anger and guilt at what has happened and an honest appraisal of his actions. It is surely impossible not to be moved when he pictures Mercutio's soul 'but a little way above our heads' (III.1.127). Thus we know *why* he has forgotten 'the reason that I have to love thee' (III.1.61), but that is not the same as saying it is right to forget it. Indeed, it is not long before Romeo himself describes his action as an error, talking of his 'cursèd hand' that 'Murdered her kinsman' (III.3.104–105). It is likely that, given more time for reflection about what happened, Romeo would have left Tybalt to the law to take care of.

Of course, while the double death in Act III scene 1 is a major factor in the plot of the play, it is by no means the only reason for the tragedy. Almost every one of the other elements that make up the final tragic compound contain similar aspects of human failings rather than fate. The fact that Capulet not only goes back on his initial intention that:

> My will to her consent is but a part,
> And, she agreed, within her scope of choice
> Lies my consent and fair according voice

(I.2.17–19)

but he also brings the date of the marriage forward simply out of relief that she is suddenly willing to consent to it. It is a decision that has far graver consequences than anyone can imagine at the time. In that sense it *is* unfortunate, but in no other sense can the decision be seen as one deriving from anything except basic human failings. After all, both the Nurse and Lady Capulet, who is herself displeased at Juliet's refusal, have earlier warned Capulet that he is 'too hot' (III.5.175), which suggests that Capulet's behaviour is very much to blame.

Even relatively minor parts of the action must be regarded in the same light. It has already been noted that we are encouraged to see the Apothecary as a decent man driven by

'Need and oppression' (V.1.70), but that doesn't make his provision of poison right. It is worth noting, too, that the letter from Friar Laurence to Romeo, explaining what Juliet has done, is not delayed by accident in any proper sense of the word. What makes it seem accidental is that the causes have no real connection with the events of the play itself. But Friar John has been deliberately prevented from making the journey, and the refusal of others to carry the letter is also no accident: the acid test is whether the response would have been the same on another occasion, and fear of the plague is always likely to produce such reactions. The failure to deliver the letter, it must be remembered, is the final seal on the deaths of the two lovers.

In this context, the opening scene of the play is, as always, important. In this case, the squabbling servants have little relevance to the plot, save to make explicit both the troubled atmosphere in which Romeo and Juliet have to love and the Prince's absolute ban on disturbance of the peace. By the same token, it is hard to feel that Gregory, Sampson and Abram are much to blame for what goes on. They are merely taking their cue from their masters, and anyway the whole sequence is almost too comic for concepts like blame. Even so, it is important to note that the notion that such a fight could be fated is still less apposite to the circumstances. The fight happens because people are seeking it.

There is, then, a human agency clearly visible in the majority of the events in *Romeo and Juliet*. More importantly, the nature of that human agency falls into something of a pattern in that the traits which are displayed can be divided largely into two areas. The first of these is obvious enough, but none the worse, perhaps, for being made explicit. Much of the action in the play derives from too great a sense of pride. If it were not the case about the 'Ancient grudge' (Prologue, line 3) that 'but their children's end, naught could remove' (Prologue, line 11), then the lovers' story would not have to be 'death-marked' (Prologue, line 9). It is surely no coincidence that our first introduction to the feud — the servants' brawl — is one which serves to heighten our sense of its absurdity and emptiness. What is more, Tybalt's arrival on the scene suggests that he at least is no better than the servants:

What, drawn, and talk of peace? I hate the word
As I hate hell, all Montagues, and thee.

(I.1.69–70)

His behaviour in the remainder of the play only goes to confirm that this kind of posturing pride is deeply suspect. This is so even when such pride is exhibited in a more moderate fashion. Thus Lady Capulet, admittedly deeply upset by Tybalt's death, cannot accept Benvolio's honest account of what has taken place, but prefers to believe that 'Some twenty of them fought in this black strife' (III.1.178), so that she can demand Romeo's life.

In fact, a slightly different sort of pride, but one equally dangerous, is the root cause of the sorry events in Act III scene 1. Mercutio, already incensed by Tybalt's insolence, is outraged at Romeo's 'calm, dishonourable, vile submission' (III.1.72) and feels that he must stand up for Romeo's honour, if Romeo will not do so himself. Of course, Tybalt would probably be less ready to insult Romeo and his friends did he not have an inflated idea of 'the injuries/ That thou hast done me' (III.1.65–66). By the same token, although here our response is almost entirely sympathetic, much the same motivation lies behind Romeo's fight with Tybalt: he is responding to the knowledge that 'My very friend hath got this mortal hurt/ In my behalf' (III.1.110–111) and that he himself has been 'effeminate' (III.1.114).

Pride is also clearly visible in Capulet's reaction to Juliet's initial refusal to marry Paris: he is piqued that far from being thanked for the arrangement, he is refused. Moreover, it is certainly arguable that his final, fatal decision to bring the date of the marriage forward is caused by his pride being pandered to by Juliet's submission in Act IV scene 2. 'This is as't should be' (IV.2.29) he says. At the other extreme, the fact that Romeo is able to obtain his poison is due largely to the fact that the Apothecary has lost all pride through deprivation. Thus the play suggests that some pride in oneself and one's position is necessary to prevent dishonourable behaviour, but that, paradoxically, too much pride also tends to provoke shabby conduct.

The other great human failing which acts as a mainspring for the action of the play is impatience. I have already discussed the way the play creates for us a sense of the sheer youth of the main participants, and with such youth goes a reluctance to wait. This is most strongly seen in Romeo, who admits 'I stand on sudden haste' (II.3.89). His revenge for Mercutio is also impetuous, and he is soon to offer to stab himself (III.3.108, stage direction) in an equally rash frenzy of remorse. Indeed, as the play moves to its climax, Balthasar still has to urge Romeo to 'have patience' (V.1.27) and Romeo doesn't wait for a letter from Friar Laurence, although he expects one.

Such impatience is seen also in Tybalt's willingness to spoil his family feast in order to overcome the shame of Romeo's being there. And, despite what I have said about the adolescent dimension to the fault, impatience is by no means confined to the younger generation in the play. Capulet, in particular, is a walking emblem of quick temper and a tendency to make snap decisions. The quality is, of course, chiefly evident in the matter of Juliet's marriage, but fairly consistently he is portrayed as a man who makes up his mind quickly and who is easily angered if anyone goes against that decision.

There is also another, more generalised aspect to the idea of impatience as it is revealed in the play: it is the way that characters jump to conclusions, making far too little effort to find out the full picture. From the moment that Tybalt assumes that Benvolio is involved in a brawl with 'these heartless hinds' (I.1.65) to that when Paris guesses that Romeo is 'come to do some villainous shame/ To the dead bodies' (V.3.52–53), we are constantly presented with characters misreading the situation, because they take too little time to ascertain the facts. It never occurs to Mercutio to wonder why Romeo is so submissive to Tybalt, offering him love for his insults: he assumes he knows enough. The tendency is one that Juliet is able to exploit; when she seems to change her mind about marrying Paris, she can be confident that her father will not enquire deeply into the new attitude. And Friar John is prevented from delivering the crucial letter to Romeo because he and his companion are *suspected* of being in a house where there is the plague.

Romeo and Juliet offers us plenty of reasons for viewing the tragedy as having essentially human causes. Indeed, as well as the two main human weaknesses that I have just outlined, I would argue that the frequent references to fate in the play only serve to illustrate another. It is somehow comforting to feel that events are beyond our control: at least we don't have to take responsibility for them. It is perhaps a little curious that the idea that we are powerless to control our existences is less frightening than the alternative, that we have to exercise such control ourselves, but in many ways this is the case. Why else would the audience of *Romeo and Juliet* seize on those aspects of the play which suggest that the whole story was fated and ignore the substantial body of evidence which shows that the causes really lie within the characters? In particular, where *Romeo and Juliet* discomforts us is the fact discussed earlier that there is no single, clear focus for blame. No one is very bad, and everyone is a little bit to blame, which is a view of life that is actually a great deal more realistic and disconcerting than that found in Shakespeare's major tragedies.

AFTERTHOUGHTS

1

Do you agree that Friar Laurence is the 'repository' of much of the play's 'wisdom, sympathy and understanding' (page 96)?

2

Does a tragedy need a villain (see page 97)?

3

Do you agree with Alton that the 'two main human weaknesses' (page 102) shown in *Romeo and Juliet* are pride and impatience?

4

How do you react to the final paragraph of this essay?

Marilyn Powrie

Marilyn Powrie has a degree in English from the University of Wales, and extensive experience in the field of literary criticism.

ESSAY

The language of love

This essay will explore, through close and detailed textual reading of selected passages, the ways in which the experience of love in Shakespeare's *Romeo and Juliet* is presented through a range of different types of poetic language. I recognise that dramatic language is always in some senses 'about itself'; that a play or poem is constantly inviting the reader to examine the medium of language rather than to accept language as a statement about something that lies beyond it, as a transparent window onto reality. I will nonetheless be arguing a somewhat unfashionable case, that the language of *Romeo and Juliet* makes firm and clear distinctions between feelings and responses that can be adjudged as 'real', or 'true', or 'natural'; and emotional experiences which the reader is encouraged to regard as 'inauthentic', 'false' or 'artificial'.

The first sustained development of a language of love begins in the first scene of the play, when Lady Montague requests news of Romeo from Benvolio. Benvolio reports seeing Romeo wandering in a nearby wood in the early morning, romantically alone, and withdrawing when his friend appears. Benvolio's speech (I.1.118–130) begins with a reference to the sunrise — 'the worshipped sun/ Peered forth the golden window of the East' — though he is talking about setting out an hour before dawn, driven by a 'troubled mind'. Though Benvolio speaks of himself as 'weary' and shunning society, that touch of poetic eloquence describing the sunrise suggests that he draws the daylight with him as he approaches Romeo. Romeo's withdrawal into the 'covert of the wood' is therefore suggested as a shunning of daylight, a retreat into the darkness of solitude and unhappiness.

Romeo's father Montague continues this imagery of light and darkness in a further series of metaphors from nature: Romeo augments the morning dew with his tears, adds to the clouds 'more clouds with his deep sighs' (lines 132–133).

> But all so soon as the all-cheering sun
> Should in the farthest East begin to draw
> The shady curtains from Aurora's bed,
> Away from light steals home my heavy son
> And private in his chamber pens himself,
> Shuts up his windows, locks fair daylight out,
> And makes himself an artificial night.
>
> (lines 134–140)

Here the sunlight referred to by Benvolio as 'worshipped' is confirmed by Montague as 'all-cheering', a source of life, vitality, regeneration. Again Romeo is described as retreating from the dawn, locking himself into a dark chamber where the daylight is unnaturally excluded. Montague's pun on 'sun/son' emphasises an unnatural opposition: the sun is 'light' (bright/not heavy) where Romeo (Montague's 'son') is 'heavy' (miserable). Despite the similarity of the two words (spelt in the sixteenth century as 'sunne' and 'sonne') there is here an unnatural relationship of opposition between the young man and the natural source of light: Romeo too should be 'light' (active, lively) rather than 'heavy'.

The text places a strong emphasis on the word 'artificial' (line 140), to strengthen the pattern of oppositions established by the verse: sunshine/clouds, natural/artificial, light/darkness (and in Elizabethan English light/heavy). In his next speech, Montague develops this pattern by adding other pairs of opposites — openness/secrecy, healthy/sick, growing/decaying. Romeo is:

> . . . to himself so secret and so close,
> So far from sounding and discovery,

As is the bud bit with an envious worm
Ere he can spread his sweet leaves to the air
Or dedicate his beauty to the sun.

(lines 149–153)

Where Romeo should be open and confiding, he is secretive and withdrawn. The secret of his emotional state is thus buried deep, beyond discovery, like the parasite which inwardly devours the flower's bud. Where he should be growing and flourishing in the sunlight, Romeo is languishing and decaying in darkness.

The characters who thus discuss Romeo's emotional condition do not identify it as love. Nonetheless, the pattern of imagery established in that opening conversation is abundantly confirmed by the language with which Romeo on his first appearance speaks of his love for Rosaline:

Why then, O brawling love, O loving hate,
O anything, of nothing first create!
O heavy lightness, serious vanity,
Misshapen chaos of well-seeming forms,
Feather of lead, bright smoke, cold fire, sick
health,
Still-waking sleep, that is not what it is!

(lines 176–181)

The opening discussion between the Montague parents and Benvolio preserved clear distinctions between opposites which Romeo here confuses and confounds. From that earlier dialogue the reader draws a confirmation of the common-sense view that light and darkness, health and sickness, nature and artifice, are entirely different things, whose oppositions should be maintained stable in a healthy life or an ordered society. Romeo's speech systematically confuses those distinctions, defining love as a chaotic force of subversion which throws all natural differences into an unruly disorder. Love is a 'heavy lightness', a 'serious vanity', a 'misshapen chaos' of 'well-seeming forms'. Lost in this emotional chaos, the lover cannot tell the difference between the serious and the frivolous, the important and the trivial, the natural and the unnatural.

This kind of poetic language clearly announces its own artificiality, and thereby throws into question the reality of the emotion it expresses. We cannot imagine, in the concrete experience of the senses, what a 'cold fire', or a 'feather of lead' could be like: the opposites cancel one another out and convey no solid meaning, only a confused distortion of reality. From a psychological point of view, Romeo may well be expressing very accurately the way he feels. But by failing to construct a tangible 'objective correlative' for love, his language clearly demonstrates that this type of love could produce nothing more than a turgid confusion of emotions: it could not conceivably become the basis for a relationship with another person.

And of course Rosaline is not really 'another person' in the play: she never appears, her existence confined to a name on a party invitation. Juliet, however, does appear, and proves very definitely to be 'another person', one whose existence declares an unmistakable human reality. Immediately Romeo catches sight of her, his language undergoes a poetic revolution:

> O, she doth teach the torches to burn bright!
> It seems she hangs upon the cheek of night
> As a rich jewel in an Ethiop's ear —
> Beauty too rich for use, for earth too dear!
> So shows a snowy dove trooping with crows
> As yonder lady o'er her fellows shows.

> (1.5.44–49)

Those features of this poetry which contrast most sharply with the language of Romeo's love for Rosaline are its celebration of light, and its extraordinary vividness and precision of sensuous detail. The young man previously noted for his avoidance of light is here converted to a rapt admirer of brilliance and illumination — the brightness of torches, the shimmering of a precious stone, the clear whiteness of a 'snowy dove'.

But there is more in this poetry than a sudden preference for light over darkness. Each figure Romeo uses is a clear, hard, distinct and tangible image, visually precise, sensuously defined, concretely imagined. Juliet's presence extinguishes the light of the torches, leaving her beauty to illuminate itself against a dark background. Her brightness stands out by contrast, as the brilliance of a jewel is set off against black skin. That distinction moves then to a contrast of outstanding clarity in the image of a white dove standing out from a troop of black crows. Romeo's poetry has thus become committed to a normative celebration of light over against darkness; each image of light or whiteness is clearly imagined with hard-edged, sensuous definition; the relationship between the sequence of images is logical and disciplined. The eloquence of this poetry rests in its firm and sure yet delicate grasp of particulars. It is the expression of an imagination moved and inspired, but not overwhelmed, by what it apprehends; moved to that kind of creative cooperation with the impact upon oneself of another's being that goes by the shorthand of 'love at first sight'. This is a poetry that shows the mind grasping, embracing and celebrating reality; not dissolving into a chaotic confusion of contradictory emotions, but seeing and feeling with emotional clarity and full experiential knowledge.

Romeo achieves this grasp of reality as a sudden revelation, prompted by the appearance of Juliet. He does not however immediately adopt this language of real love as an altered perspective on the world. On the contrary, once engaged in dialogue with Juliet in the 'balcony scene', Romeo's language seems to revert to the irrational artifice of his earlier utterances. His famous address to Juliet as he sees her at the window from the darkness of Capulet's orchard (II.2.1–32) is of course a sustained invocation of light, continuous with his previous speech at the ball. Juliet is here seen as the sun, her eyes as stars, her presence bright as that of an angel. But this impassioned romantic eloquence is jolted into sudden relief by the intrusion of another language, an accent of extraordinary directness and common sense:

> O Romeo, Romeo! — wherefore art thou Romeo?
> Deny thy father and refuse thy name.
> Or, if thou wilt not, be but sworn my love,
> And I'll no longer be a Capulet.

> (II.2.33–36)

The common misreading of that first line (it is usually interpreted to mean 'where are you, Romeo?', when the true meaning is 'why are you Romeo [i.e. a Montague]?'), suggests on Juliet's part a vague romantic yearning which is quite foreign to her language of love. On the contrary, her attention is firmly and sharply focused on the real social conditions that form obstacles to their union — the feud between their respective families. Love, for Juliet, is certainly not blind: her almost prosaic poetry mediates effectively between romantic eloquence — 'Romeo, doff thy name;/ And for thy name, which is no part of thee,/ Take all myself' (lines 47–49) — and a clearsighted grasp of reality. The ensuing dialogue draws a continual contrast between Romeo's reversion to idealised romantic sentiment, and Juliet's reasoned, practical vigilance towards the real:

> JULIET How camest thou hither, tell me, and wherefore?
> . . .
> ROMEO With love's light wings did I o'erperch these walls.
>
> (II.2.62, 66)

Where Juliet asks specific, practical questions, and alerts Romeo to real dangers, his language effuses that same conviction of a fundamental opposition between love and reality that characterised the language of his love for Rosaline.

It is through Juliet's speech that the play offers the possibility of a genuine language of love, in which there is no irreconcilable contradiction between the opposites of light and darkness, the natural and the artificial, dream and reality. I have been speaking of Juliet's language as if it were a kind of prose, alert to the nature of material reality but deaf to the rich textures of a more impassioned, romantic poetry. In fact, Juliet can speak all the languages of love, and it is under her tutelage that Romeo learns, albeit for a brief season, to hold together in language the antinomies of experience. Waiting in her chamber for Romeo, the newly wedded Juliet begins in a declamatory style full of classical allusions:

> Gallop apace, you fiery-footed steeds,
> Towards Phoebus' lodging! Such a waggoner
> As Phaëton would whip you to the West
> And bring in cloudy night immediately.
>
> (III.2.1–4)

This longing for the coming of night is the opposite of the light-shunning withdrawal we saw in Romeo at the play's outset; for this is a darkness brilliantly illuminated by the light of love:

> Lovers can see to do their amorous rites

By their own beauties . . .

(lines 8–9)

Eloquent and elevated though this love poetry is, it is not incompatible in Juliet's speech with the down-to-earth expression of simple and natural emotion:

> So tedious is this day
> As is the night before some festival
> To an impatient child that hath new robes
> And may not wear them.

(lines 28–31)

Such detailed observation from common life immeasurably enriches the high romantic emotion with which the speech began: beside the eloquence of the tragic heroine is set the impatience of the little girl eager to wear her new dress before the party.

The tragedy of *Romeo and Juliet* could be described as a loss of language. The poetry of Juliet offers the powerful possibility of an integrated speech capable of ordering the world, just as the lovers offer Verona an opportunity of redemption through love. Verona of course declines the offer, and the lovers die. As a commemorative statue erected by her mourning parents at the end of the play, Juliet retains her beauty and romantic elevation. Her speech, with its unique and irreplaceable mastery of reality, is however silenced for ever.

Or until the play is read or performed again. An appropriate epitaph for Juliet could perhaps be found in Shakespeare's Sonnet 18:

> So long as men can breathe, or eyes can see,
> So long lives this, and this gives life to thee.

AFTERTHOUGHTS

1

What do you understand by 'objective correlative' (page 108)?

2

Trace the significance to Powrie's argument of her analysis of light/dark imagery.

3

Compare and contrast the argument of this essay with the essay by Mangan (pages 63–73).

4

What has drawn so many contributors to this volume to Sonnet 18?

INTRODUCTION

First, a word of warning. Good essays are the product of a creative engagement with literature. So never try to restrict your studies to what you think will be 'useful in the exam'. Ironically, you will restrict your grade potential if you do.

This doesn't mean, of course, that you should ignore the basic skills of essay writing. When you read critics, make a conscious effort to notice *how* they communicate their ideas. The guidelines that follow offer advice of a more explicit kind. But they are no substitute for practical experience. It is never easy to express ideas with clarity and precision. But the more often you tackle the problems involved and experiment to find your own voice, the more fluent you will become. So practise writing essays as often as possible.

HOW TO PLAN
AN ESSAY

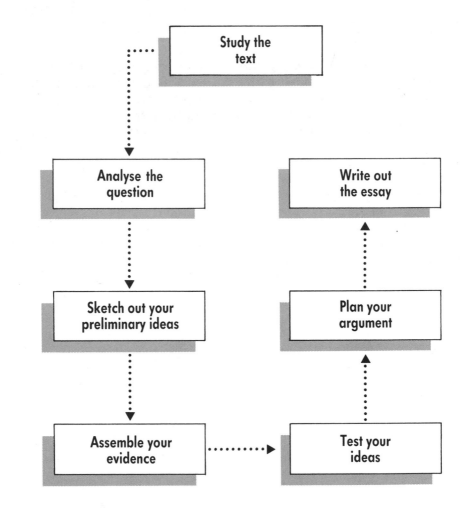

Study the
text

Analyse the
question

Write out
the essay

Sketch out your
preliminary ideas

Plan your
argument

Assemble your
evidence

Test your
ideas

Study the text

The first step in writing a good essay is to get to know the set text well. Never write about a text until you are fully familiar with it. Even a discussion of the opening chapter of a novel, for example, should be informed by an understanding of the book as a whole. Literary texts, however, are by their very nature complex and on a first reading you are bound to miss many significant features. Re-read the book with care, if possible more than once. Look up any unfamiliar words in a good dictionary and if the text you are studying was written more than a few decades ago, consult the *Oxford English Dictionary* to find out whether the meanings of any terms have shifted in the intervening period.

Good books are difficult to put down when you first read them. But a more leisurely second or third reading gives you the opportunity to make notes on those features you find significant. An index of characters and events is often useful, particularly when studying novels with a complex plot or time scheme. The main aim, however, should be to record your *responses* to the text. By all means note, for example, striking images. But be sure to add *why* you think them striking. Similarly, record any thoughts you may have on interesting comparisons with other texts, puzzling points of characterisation, even what you take to be aesthetic blemishes. The important thing is to annotate fully and adventurously. The most seemingly idiosyncratic comment may later lead to a crucial area of discussion which you would otherwise have overlooked. It helps to have a working copy of the text in which to mark up key passages and jot down marginal comments (although obviously these practices are taboo when working with library, borrowed or valuable copies!). But keep a fuller set of notes as well and organise these under appropriate headings.

Literature does not exist in an aesthetic vacuum, however, and you should try to find out as much as possible about the context of its production and reception. It is particularly important to read other works by the same author and writings by contemporaries. At this early stage, you may want to restrict your secondary reading to those standard reference works, such as biographies, which are widely available in public libraries. In the long run, however, it pays to read as wide a range of critical studies as possible.

Some students, and tutors, worry that such studies may stifle the development of any truly personal response. But this won't happen if you are alert to the danger and read critically. After all, you wouldn't passively accept what a stranger told you in conversation. The fact that a critic's views are in print does not necessarily make them any more authoritative (as a glance at the review pages of the *TLS* and *London Review of Books* will reveal). So question the views you find: 'Does this critic's interpretation agree with mine and where do we part company?' 'Can it be right to try and restrict this text's meanings to those found by its author or first audience?' 'Doesn't this passage treat a theatrical text as though it were a novel?' Often it is views which you reject which prove most valuable since they challenge you to articulate your own position with greater clarity. Be sure to keep careful notes on what the critic wrote, and your *reactions* to what the critic wrote.

Analyse the question

You cannot begin to answer a question until you understand what task it is you have been asked to perform. Recast the question in your own words and reconstruct the line of reasoning which lies behind it. Where there is a choice of topics, try to choose the one for which you are best prepared. It would, for example, be unwise to tackle 'How far do you agree that in *Paradise Lost* Milton transformed the epic models he inherited from ancient Greece and Rome?' without a working knowledge of Homer and Virgil (or *Paradise Lost* for that matter!). If you do not already know the works of these authors, the question should spur you on to read more widely — or discourage you from attempting it at all. The scope of an essay, however, is not always so obvious and you must remain alert to the implied demands of each question. How could you possibly 'Consider the view that *Wuthering Heights* transcends the conventions of the Gothic novel' without reference to at least some of those works which, the question suggests, have *not* transcended Gothic conventions?

When you have decided on a topic, analyse the terms of the question itself. Sometimes these self-evidently require careful definition: *tragedy* and *irony*, for example, are notoriously difficult concepts to pin down and you will probably need to consult a good dictionary of literary terms. Don't ignore, however, those seemingly innocuous phrases which often smuggle in significant assumptions. 'Does Macbeth lack the nobility of the true tragic hero?' obviously invites you to discuss nobility and the nature of the tragic hero. But what of 'lack' and 'true' — do they suggest that the play would be improved had Shakespeare depicted Macbeth in a different manner? or that tragedy is superior to other forms of drama? Remember that you are not expected meekly to agree with the assumptions implicit in the question. Some questions are deliberately provocative in order to stimulate an engaged response. Don't be afraid to take up the challenge.

Sketch out your preliminary ideas

'Which comes first, the evidence or the answer?' is one of those chicken and egg questions. How can you form a view without inspecting the evidence? But how can you know which evidence is relevant without some idea of what it is you are looking for? In practice the mind reviews evidence and formulates preliminary theories or hypotheses at one and the same time, although for the sake of clarity we have separated out the processes. Remember that these early ideas are only there to get you started. You *expect* to modify them in the light of the evidence you uncover. Your initial hypothesis may be an instinctive 'gut-reaction'. Or you may find that you prefer to 'sleep on the problem', allowing ideas to gell over a period of time. Don't worry in either case. The mind is quite capable of processing a vast amount of accumulated evidence, the product of previous reading and thought, and reaching sophisticated intuitive judgements. Eventually, however, you are going to have to think carefully through any ideas you arrive at by such intuitive processes. Are they logical? Do they take account of all the relevant factors? Do they fully answer the question set? Are there any obvious reasons to qualify or abandon them?

Assemble your evidence

Now is the time to return to the text and re-read it with the question and your working hypothesis firmly in mind. Many of the notes you have already made are likely to be useful, but assess the precise relevance of this material and make notes on any new evidence you discover. The important thing is to cast your net widely and take into account points which tend to undermine your case as well as those that support it. As always, ensure that your notes are full, accurate, and reflect your own critical judgements.

You may well need to go outside the text if you are to do full justice to the question. If you think that the 'Oedipus complex' may be relevant to an answer on *Hamlet* then read Freud and a balanced selection of those critics who have discussed the appropriateness of applying psychoanalytical theories to the interpretation of literature. Their views can most easily be tracked down by consulting the annotated bibliographies held by most major libraries (and don't be afraid to ask a librarian for help in finding and using these). Remember that you go to works of criticism not only to obtain information but to stimulate you into clarifying your own position. And that since life is short and many critical studies are long, judicious use of a book's index and/or contents list is not to be scorned. You can save yourself a great deal of future labour if you carefully record full bibliographic details at this stage.

Once you have collected the evidence, organise it coherently. Sort the detailed points into related groups and identify the quotations which support these. You must also assess the relative importance of each point, for in an essay of limited length it is essential to establish a firm set of priorities, exploring some ideas in depth while discarding or subordinating others.

Test your ideas

As we stressed earlier, a hypothesis is only a proposal, and one that you fully expect to modify. Review it with the evidence before you. Do you really still believe in it? It would be surprising if you did not want to modify it in some way. If you cannot see any problems, others may. Try discussing your ideas with friends and relatives. Raise them in class discussions. Your tutor is certain to welcome your initiative. The critical process is essentially collaborative and there is absolutely no reason why you should not listen to and benefit from the views of others. Similarly, you should feel free to test your ideas against the theories put forward in academic journals and books. But do not just borrow what you find. Critically analyse the views on offer and, where appropriate, integrate them into your own pattern of thought. You must, of course, give full acknowledgement to the sources of such views.

Do not despair if you find you have to abandon or modify significantly your initial position. The fact that you are prepared to do so is a mark of intellectual integrity. Dogmatism is never an academic virtue and many of the best essays explore the *process* of scholarly enquiry rather than simply record its results.

Plan your argument

Once you have more or less decided on your attitude to the question (for an answer is never really 'finalised') you have to present your case in the most persuasive manner. In order to do this you must avoid meandering from point to point and instead produce an organised argument — a structured flow of ideas and supporting evidence, leading logically to a conclusion which fully answers the question. Never begin to write until you have produced an outline of your argument.

You may find it easiest to begin by sketching out its main stage as a flow chart or some other form of visual presentation. But eventually you should produce a list of paragraph topics. The paragraph is the conventional written demarcation for a unit of thought and you can outline an argument quite simply by briefly summarising the substance of each paragraph and then checking that these points (you may remember your English teacher referring to them as topic sentences) really do follow a coherent order. Later you will be able to elaborate on each topic, illustrating and qualifying it as you go along. But you will find this far easier to do if you possess from the outset a clear map of where you are heading.

All questions require some form of an argument. Even so-called 'descriptive' questions *imply* the need for an argument. An adequate answer to the request to 'Outline the role of Iago in *Othello*' would do far more than simply list his appearances on stage. It would at the very least attempt to provide some *explanation* for his actions — is he, for example, a representative stage 'Machiavel'? an example of pure evil, 'motiveless malignity'? or a realistic study of a tormented personality reacting to identifiable social and psychological pressures?

Your conclusion ought to address the terms of the question. It may seem obvious, but 'how far do you agree', 'evaluate', 'consider', 'discuss', etc, are *not* interchangeable formulas and your conclusion must take account of the precise wording of the question. If asked 'How far do you agree?', the concluding paragraph of your essay really should state whether you are in complete agreement, total disagreement, or, more likely, partial agreement. Each preceding paragraph should have a clear justification for its existence and help to clarify the reasoning which underlies your conclusion. If you find that a paragraph serves no good purpose (perhaps merely summarising the plot), do not hesitate to discard it.

The arrangement of the paragraphs, the overall strategy of the argument, can vary. One possible pattern is dialectical: present the arguments in favour of one point of view (**thesis**); then turn to counter-arguments or to a rival interpretation (**antithesis**); finally evaluate the competing claims and arrive at your own conclusion (**synthesis**). You may, on the other hand, feel so convinced of the merits of one particular case that you wish to devote your entire essay to arguing that viewpoint persuasively (although it is always desirable to indicate, however briefly, that you are aware of alternative, if flawed, positions). As the essays contained in this volume demonstrate, there are many other possible strategies. Try to adopt the one which will most comfortably accommodate the demands of the question and allow you to express your thoughts with the greatest possible clarity.

Be careful, however, not to apply abstract formulas in a mechanical manner. It is true that you should be careful to define your terms. It is *not* true that every essay should begin with 'The dictionary defines *x* as . . .'. In fact, definitions are often best left until an appropriate moment for their introduction arrives. Similarly every essay should have a beginning, middle and end. But it does not follow that in your opening paragraph you should announce an intention to write an essay, or that in your concluding paragraph you need to signal an imminent desire to put down your pen. The old adages are often useful reminders of what constitutes good practice, but they must be interpreted intelligently.

Write out the essay

Once you have developed a coherent argument you should aim to communicate it in the most effective manner possible. Make certain you clearly identify yourself, and the question you are answering. Ideally, type your answer, or at least ensure your handwriting is legible and that you leave sufficient space for your tutor's comments. Careless presentation merely distracts from the force of your argument. Errors of grammar, syntax and spelling are far more serious. At best they are an irritating blemish, particularly in the work of a student who should be sensitive to the nuances of language. At worst, they seriously confuse the sense of your argument. If you are aware that you have stylistic problems of this kind, ask your tutor for advice at the earliest opportunity. Everyone, however, is liable to commit the occasional howler. The only remedy is to give yourself plenty of time in which to proof-read your manuscript (often reading it aloud is helpful) before submitting it.

Language, however, is not only an instrument of communication; it is also an instrument of thought. If you want to think clearly and precisely you should strive for a clear, precise prose style. Keep your sentences short and direct. Use modern, straightforward English wherever possible. Avoid repetition, clichés and wordiness. Beware of generalisations, simplifications, and overstatements. Orwell analysed the relationship between stylistic vice and muddled thought in his essay 'Politics and the English Language' (1946) — it remains essential reading (and is still readily available in volume 4 of the Penguin *Collected Essays, Journalism and Letters*). Generalisations, for example, are always dangerous. They are rarely true and tend to suppress the individuality of the texts in question. A remark such as 'Keats always employs sensuous language in his poetry' is not only fatuous (what, after all, does it mean? is *every* word he wrote equally 'sensuous'?) but tends to obscure interesting distinctions which could otherwise be made between, say, the descriptions in the 'Ode on a Grecian Urn' and those in 'To Autumn'.

The intelligent use of quotations can help you make your points with greater clarity. Don't sprinkle them throughout your essay without good reason. There is no need, for example, to use them to support uncontentious statements of fact. 'Macbeth murdered Duncan' does not require textual evidence (unless you wish to dispute Thurber's brilliant parody, 'The Great Macbeth Murder Mystery', which reveals Lady Macbeth's father as the culprit!). Quotations should be included, however, when they are necessary to support your case. The proposition that Macbeth's imaginative powers wither after he has killed his king would certainly require extensive quotation: you would almost certainly want to analyse key passages from both before and after the murder (perhaps his first and last soliloquies?). The key word here is 'analyse'. Quotations cannot make your points on their own. It is up to you to demonstrate their relevance and clearly explain to your readers *why* you want them to focus on the passage you have selected.

Most of the academic conventions which govern the presentation of essays are set out briefly in the style sheet below. The question of gender, however, requires fuller discussion. More than half the population of the world is female, yet many writers still refer to an undifferentiated *man*kind. Or write of the author and *his* public. We do not think that this convention has much to recommend it. At the very least, it runs the risk of introducing unintended sexist attitudes. And at times leads to such patent absurdities as 'Cleopatra's final speech asserts *man*'s true nobility'. With a little thought, you can normally find ways of expressing yourself which do not suggest that the typical author, critic or reader is male. Often you can simply use plural forms, which is probably a more elegant solution than relying on such awkward formulations as 's/he' or 'he and she'. You should also try to avoid distinguishing between male and female authors on the basis of forenames. Why *Jane* Austen and not *George* Byron? Refer to all authors by their last names unless there is some good reason not to. Where there may otherwise be confusion, say between T S and George Eliot, give the name in full when if first occurs and thereafter use the last name only.

Finally, keep your audience firmly in mind. Tutors and examiners are interested in understanding your conclusions and the processes by which you arrived at them. They are not interested in reading a potted version of a book they already know. **So don't pad out your work with plot summary.**

Hints for examinations

In an examination you should go through exactly the same processes as you would for the preparation of a term essay. The only difference lies in the fact that some of the stages will have had to take place before you enter the examination room. This should not bother you unduly. Examiners are bound to avoid the merely eccentric when they come to formulate papers and if you have read widely and thought deeply about the central issues raised by your set texts you can be confident you will have sufficient material to answer the majority of questions sensibly.

The fact that examinations impose strict time limits makes it *more*, rather than less, important that you plan carefully. There really is no point in floundering into an answer without any idea of where you are going, particularly when there will not be time to recover from the initial error.

Before you begin to answer any question at all, study the entire paper with care. Check that you understand the rubric and know how many questions you have to answer and whether any are compulsory. It may be comforting to spot a title you feel confident of answering well, but don't rush to tackle it: read *all* the questions before deciding which *combination* will allow you to display your abilities to the fullest advantage. Once you have made your choice, analyse each question, sketch out your ideas, assemble the evidence, review your initial hypothesis, plan your argument, *before* trying to write out an answer. And make notes at each stage: not only will these help you arrive at a sensible conclusion, but examiners are impressed by evidence of careful thought.

Plan your time as well as your answers. If you have practised writing timed essays as part of your revision, you should not find this too difficult. There can be a temptation to allocate extra time to the questions you know you can answer well; but this is always a short-sighted policy. You will find yourself left to face a question which would in any event have given you difficulty without even the time to give it serious thought. It is, moreover, easier to gain marks at the lower end of the scale than at the upper, and you will never compensate for one poor answer by further polishing two satisfactory answers. Try to leave some time at the end of the examination to re-read your answers and correct any obvious errors. If the worst comes to the worst and you run short of time, don't just keep writing until you are forced to break off in mid-paragraph. It is far better to provide for the examiner a set of notes which indicate the overall direction of your argument.

Good luck — but if you prepare for the examination conscientiously and tackle the paper in a methodical manner, you won't need it!

short prose quotation incorporated in the text of the essay, within quotation marks.

long verse quotation indented and introduced by a colon. No quotation marks are needed.

Three dots (ellipsis) indicate where words or phrases have been cut from a quotation or where (as here) a quotation begins mid-sentence.

Line reference given directly after the quotation, in brackets.

book/play titles are given in italics. In a handwritten or typed manuscript this would appear as underlining: King Lear; Othello.

Short verse quotation incorporated in the text of the essay within quotation marks. If the quotation ran on into a second line of poetry, this would be indicated by a slash (/).

deceiving Benedick and Beatrice into 'a mountain of affection th'one with th'other' (II.1.339–340). The basis of both plots is getting the victims to overhear other people speaking, as they think, honestly.

In fact, therefore, we are being presented with two types of deceit: that which is benevolent, like Don Pedro's or the Friar's seeking ultimately a harmony that can be expressed marriage, and that which is totally destructive, like Don J The success of each type of deceit depends on a manipul language and an alteration of behaviour and appearances n the readiness of the victims to judge from what is pres their eyes and ears. Telling the two types apart may ult.

t is not as if any character is unaware of the difficult ionship of appearance to reality: but nearly every one is led hoose, of two alternatives, the wrong one. The best instance of this comes at the crisis of the play:

HERO   . . . seemed I ever otherwise to you?
CLAUDIO Out of thee! Seeming! I will write against it.
         You seem to me as Dian in her orb,
         As chaste as is the bud ere it be blown;
         But you are more intemperate in your blood
         Than Venus, or those pampered animals
         That rage in savage sensuality.

                                        (IV.1.53–59)

Hero's innocent use of the word 'seemed' — not 'was' — gets Claudio on the raw, for it raises the issue of behaviour versus real nature that is the cause of his torment. It triggers remarkable anticipation of Othello's tortured animal im that highlights the emotional perception of the disju between appearance and what Claudio at this point beli be reality. He could not be more wrong; and he is wrong he trusted the suspect word of Don John and what he wa to see at Hero's window rather than the woman he chose to as his wife. Love must, as both Desdemona (*Othello*) and Cordelia (*King Lear*) know, depend on trust: it (or its lack) can never be *proved*. Claudio is given 'ocular proof' (*Othello* III.3.360) of Hero's apparent unchasti, just as Othello is of Desdemona's by Iago, a stage-managing and manipulating

125

We have divided the following information into two sections. Part A describes those rules which it is essential to master no matter what kind of essay you are writing (including examination answers). Part B sets out some of the more detailed conventions which govern the documentation of essays.

PART A: LAYOUT

Titles of texts

Titles of published books, plays (of any length), long poems, pamphlets and periodicals (including newspapers and magazines), works of classical literature, and films should be underlined: e.g. David Copperfield (novel), Twelfth Night (play), Paradise Lost (long poem), Critical Quarterly (periodical), Horace's Ars Poetica (Classical work), Apocalypse Now (film).

Notice how important it is to distinguish between titles and other names. Hamlet is the play; Hamlet the prince. Wuthering Heights is the novel; Wuthering Heights the house. Underlining is the equivalent in handwritten or typed manuscripts of printed italics. So what normally appears in this volume as *Othello* would be written as Othello in your essay.

Titles of articles, essays, short stories, short poems, songs, chapters of books, speeches, and newspaper articles are enclosed in quotation marks; e.g. 'The Flea' (short poem), 'The Prussian Officer' (short story), 'Middleton's Chess Strategies' (article), 'Thatcher Defects!' (newspaper headline).

Exceptions: Underlining titles or placing them within quotation marks does not apply to sacred writings (e.g. Bible, Koran, Old Testament, Gospels) or parts of a book (e.g. Preface, Introduction, Appendix).

It is generally incorrect to place quotation marks around a title of a published book which you have underlined. The exception is 'titles within titles': e.g. 'Vanity Fair': A Critical Study (title of a book about *Vanity Fair*).

Quotations

Short verse quotations of a single line or part of a line should be incorporated within quotation marks as part of the running text of your essay. Quotations of two or three lines of verse are treated in the same way, with line endings indicated by a slash(/). For example:

1 In <u>Julius Caesar,</u> Antony says of Brutus, 'This was the noblest Roman of them all'.

2 The opening of Antony's famous funeral oration, 'Friends, Romans, Countrymen, lend me your ears;/ I come to bury Caesar not to praise him', is a carefully controlled piece of rhetoric.

Longer verse quotations of more than three lines should be indented from the main body of the text and introduced in most cases with a colon. Do not enclose indented quotations within quotation marks. For example:

It is worth pausing to consider the reasons Brutus gives to justify his decision to assassinate Caesar:

> It must be by his death; and for my part,
> I know no personal cause to spurn at him,
> But for the general. He would be crowned.
> How might that change his nature, there's the question.

At first glance his rationale may appear logical . . .

Prose quotations of less than three lines should be incorporated in the text of the essay, within quotation marks. Longer prose quotations should be indented and the quotation marks omitted. For example:

1 Before his downfall, Caesar rules with an iron hand. His political opponents, the Tribunes Marullus and Flavius, are 'put to silence' for the trivial offence of 'pulling scarfs off Caesar's image'.

2 It is interesting to note the rhetorical structure of Brutus's Forum speech:

> Romans, countrymen, and lovers, hear me for my cause, and be silent that you may hear. Believe me for my honour, and have respect to mine honour that you may believe. Censure me in your wisdom, and awake your senses, that you may the better judge.

Tenses: When you are relating the events that occur within a work of fiction or describing the author's technique, it is the convention to use the present tense. Even though Orwell published *Animal Farm* in 1945, the book *describes* the animals' seizure of Manor Farm. Similarly, Macbeth always *murders* Duncan, despite the passage of time.

PART B: DOCUMENTATION

When quoting from verse of more than twenty lines, provide line references: e.g. In 'Upon Appleton House' Marvell's mower moves 'With whistling scythe and elbow strong' (1.393).

Quotations from plays should be identified by act, scene and line references: e.g. Prospero, in Shakespeare's The Tempest, refers to Caliban as 'A devil, a born devil' (IV.1.188). (i.e. Act 4. Scene 1. Line 188).

Quotations from prose works should provide a chapter reference and, where appropriate, a page reference.

Bibliographies should list full details of all sources consulted. The way in which they are presented varies, but one standard format is as follows:

1 Books and articles are listed in alphabetical order by the author's last name. Initials are placed after the surname.
2 If you are referring to a chapter or article within a larger work, you list it by reference to the author of the article or chapter, not the editor (although the editor is also named in the reference).
3 Give (in parentheses) the place and date of publication, e.g. (London, 1962). These details can be found within the book itself. Here are some examples:

> Brockbank, J.P., 'Shakespeare's Histories, English and Roman', in Ricks, C. (ed.) English Drama to 1710 (Sphere History of Literature in the English Language) (London, 1971).
> Gurr, A., 'Richard III and the Democratic Process', Essays in Criticism 24 (1974), pp. 39–47.
> Spivack, B., Shakespeare and the Allegory of Evil (New York, 1958).

Footnotes: In general, try to avoid using footnotes and build your references into the body of the essay wherever possible. When you do use them give the full bibliographic reference to a work in the first instance and then use a short title: e.g. See K. Smidt, Unconformities in Shakespeare's History Plays (London, 1982), pp. 43–47 becomes Smidt (pp. 43–47) thereafter. Do not use terms such as 'ibid.' or 'op. cit.' unless you are absolutely sure of their meaning.

There is a principle behind all this seeming pedantry. The reader ought to be able to find and check your references and quotations as quickly and easily as possible. Give additional information, such as canto or volume number whenever you think it will assist your reader.

SUGGESTIONS FOR FURTHER READING

Cribb, T J, 'The Unity of *Romeo and Juliet*', *Shakespeare Survey*, 34 (Cambridge, 1981)

Everett, Barbara, '*Romeo and Juliet*: the Nurse's Story', in Cox, C B, and Palmer, D J (eds), *Shakespeare's Wide and Universal Stage* (Manchester, 1984)

Frye, Northrop, '*Romeo and Juliet*', in *Northrop Frye on Shakespeare* (New York, 1986)

Holderness, G, *Romeo and Juliet: A Critical Study* (Harmondsworth, 1990)

Kahn, Coppélia, 'Coming of Age in Verona', in Lenz, C R S, Greene, G, and Neely, C T (eds), *The Woman's Part: Feminist Criticism of Shakespeare* (Illinois, 1980)

Mahood, M M, *Shakespeare's Wordplay* (London, 1957)

Snyder, Susan, *The Comic Matrix of Shakespeare's Tragedies* (Princeton, N J, 1979)

Taylor, Neil and Loughrey, Bryan (eds), *Shakespeare's Early Tragedies: A Casebook* (Basingstoke, 1990)

Watts, Cedric, *Harvester New Critical Introduction to 'Romeo and Juliet'* (Hemel Hempstead, 1990)

Longman Group UK Limited
*Longman House, Burnt Mill, Harlow, Essex, CM20 2JE, England
and Associated Companies throughout the World.*

First published 1991
ISBN 0 582 07577 7

*Set in 10/12 pt Century Schoolbook, Linotron 202
Printed in Great Britain by Bell and Bain Ltd., Glasgow*

Acknowledgement
The editors would like to thank Zachary Leader for his assistance with
the style sheet.